THREE SCREENPLAYS

LUIS BUÑUEL

THREE SCREENPLAYS

Viridiana

The Exterminating Angel

Simon of the Desert

The Orion Press   *New York*

CONTENTS

Viridiana *(1961)*

Translated by Piergiuseppe Bozzetti

Credits

Produced by Gustavo Alatriste (Mexico) and Uninci Films 59 (Madrid). Executive Producer: R. Muñoz Suay. Script by Luis Buñuel and Julio Alejandro. Music by Handel. Photographed by José A. Agayo. Décor by Francisco Canet. Edited by Pedro del Rey.

Cast

Silvia Pinal	*Viridiana*
Fernando Rey	*Don Jaime*
Francisco Rabal	*His son*
Victoria Zinny	*Lucia*
Margarita Lozano	*Ramona*
Teresa Rabal	*Rita*

The courtyard and cloister of a convent. A group of little boys walking two by two in line are led across the courtyard by some nuns. Other nuns are coming and going in the courtyard or along the cloister, where a priest is also passing.

In a corner of the courtyard a group of nuns are chatting. One of them is Viridiana. The Mother Superior comes toward her.

The film opens to the strains of Handel's Hallelujah Chorus, which accompany the credits. Then the music fades as the first picture comes on.

MOTHER SUPERIOR: Sister Viridiana.

The young nun breaks away from the group and comes toward the Mother Superior. She bows.

VIRIDIANA: Mother?

MOTHER SUPERIOR: I've just had a letter from your uncle. He won't be able to come when you take your vows.

VIRIDIANA *(indifferent)*: All right, Mother.

The Mother Superior is astonished at her lack of concern.

MOTHER SUPERIOR: You don't seem to mind very much.

Both have begun to walk along the cloister.

VIRIDIANA: I hardly know him. I saw him only once, some years ago. I can't even remember him.

MOTHER SUPERIOR: In any case he's asking you to come and stay with him.

VIRIDIANA: I don't want to leave the convent, Mother.

MOTHER SUPERIOR: I'm afraid that his health is not good. He's your only relative and you ought to say farewell to him before taking your vows. You will certainly never see him again.

They stop and face each other.

VIRIDIANA: But why does he want to see me? He has never bothered about me.

MOTHER SUPERIOR: He has paid for your studies and your

maintenance, and he has just sent your dowry. Does that mean so little to you, Viridiana?

Viridiana, taken aback, seems to reflect. They start walking again.

VIRIDIANA: I have no desire to see the world again, but if you order me to...

MOTHER SUPERIOR: The retreat will start soon. You can leave tomorrow morning. *(They stop and face each other again; Viridiana looks dejectedly at the Mother Superior.)* Everything you need for the journey has been put in your cell. Go get yourself ready, and try to show him some affection.

She smiles at her again and leaves. Viridiana, looking worried, watches her go.

Private park. Close-up of the dirty, skinny legs of little Rita, who is jumping rope. They come forward and go back, opening and shutting like compasses. Rita jumps from one bare foot to the other. Near by, behind her, the legs of a man are seen passing. As they recede, the chest, then the face, of Don Jaime appear. He watches the little girl's legs.

The head of the breathless little girl is tousled, her eyes shining and her lips moist. She bites her lower lip. Don Jaime comes toward her.

The noise of a horse and carriage stopping is heard near by. Rita stops skipping and looks toward the carriage.

DON JAIME: That's enough for today, Rita. Do you like that rope I gave you?

RITA: It's easier to jump with: it's got handles.

DON JAIME: Go away now. Go and play.

Rita hands the rope to Don Jaime, who hangs it on a nail fixed to the trunk of a big tree which overshadows them. Don Jaime then turns his attention to the carriage and begins to walk toward it. Rita also goes toward the carriage. Viridiana is getting out. The coachman hands down her small bag.

RITA: Hello.

VIRIDIANA: Hello.

RAMONA: Welcome, miss. I'm Ramona, Don Jaime's servant.

VIRIDIANA: Ah! Pleased to meet you.

Don Jaime arrives now.

DON JAIME: Viridiana!

The young girl leaves the maid and moves to face her uncle. They look at each other with curiosity. The novice's expression is what one would expect in such circumstances, but Don Jaime shows a more lively interest.

VIRIDIANA: Yes, Uncle. How are you?

DON JAIME: I'm well... The bus was late, wasn't it?... What was the journey like?

VIRIDIANA: Excellent. What a charming, peaceful place, Uncle.

DON JAIME: You'll think you're still at the convent.

In spite of a total lack of cordiality and warmth on both sides, Don Jaime's face now registers the great interest his niece has aroused in him.

The camera frames the legs of Viridiana and Don Jaime, who are moving forward side by side. They stop occasionally, as people do when they are walking and talking together. At first we only hear their voices. Then the camera shows them both completely. The tone of the conversation is normal, except that Don Jaime's voice shows evident interest. Hers has less expression.

DON JAIME: How long are you staying?

VIRIDIANA: A very short while, Uncle. I've been given permission to stay only a few days.

DON JAIME: Was that difficult to get?

VIRIDIANA: No. Mother Superior told me to come.

Don Jaime stops.

DON JAIME *(crestfallen)* : Did you have so little interest in seeing me?

VIRIDIANA *(smiling, sincere)* : To tell you the truth, not very much. I cannot lie. I respect you and I am grateful to you because I owe you everything materially, but otherwise...

DON JAIME *(sadly)* : You have no feelings toward...

VIRIDIANA : No.

They start walking again. He begins to show pleasure, as well as surprise, at the frankness of the young girl.

DON JAIME : You are right. Being alone has made me self-centered. Now I am sorry we have not seen more of each other. It's too late, isn't it?

She makes a gesture of resignation and indifference.

VIRIDIANA : Yes. It's too late.

Now they are passing under a big tree, the branches and trunk of which overshadow the two stories of the house. In the distance are the fields of the estate, lying waste and fallow.

VIRIDIANA : You've been neglecting the farm, Uncle.

DON JAIME : In twenty years the grass has invaded everything. There are spiders all over the house except on the first floor. I hardly ever go out.

RITA'S VOICE *(from the thickest part of the tree)* : It's true. When he goes out he makes me jump rope.

Astonished, Viridiana looks up into the branches. The head of the little girl appears among the leaves.

DON JAIME : Come down here, you scamp.

VIRIDIANA : Who is she?

DON JAIME : My maid Ramona's daughter. She's a little animal.

VIRIDIANA : Come down.

The little girl disappears again among the leaves. Viridiana walks on, drawing ahead of her uncle.

DON JAIME: How like your aunt you are, even in your walk.

VIRIDIANA: I know, Uncle, you've told me that already.

DON JAIME: You see, even the voice.

They walk on under the trees of the estate.

Don Jaime's sitting room at night. Close-up of Don Jaime's feet slowly working the pedals of a harmonium; his hands playing on the keyboard. He is playing a piece of classical music.

Doña Elvira's bedroom. Viridiana is undressing. She takes off her dress and then sits on the edge of the bed to take off her black stockings. Her legs, white and perfectly shaped, appear in full light.

The sitting room. Don Jaime, with an ecstatic faraway look on his face, continues to play the harmonium.

The hall. Ramona moves a few paces and stops. She hesitates for a moment, and then comes back toward Viridiana's room. She looks through the keyhole. The sound of the harmonium comes from the sitting room.

The sitting room. Don Jaime is still in his musical ecstasy. Ramona comes in and goes quietly to her master. She stops near him and for a moment watches his hands on the keys.

RAMONA: She has made her bed on the floor, sir! *(The old man continues to play without answering.)* She has something in her suitcase that looks like thorns. Her nightgown is made of some rough cloth. It really must tear her skin! *(Pause.)* Such beautiful skin, sir.

Don Jaime, his attention suddenly caught, continues to play.

DON JAIME: Leave me now. You can go to bed.

RAMONA: Yes, sir. Good night.

Don Jaime goes on playing.

Doña Elvira's bedroom. Close-up of a crucifix of rough wood, surrounded by replicas of the instruments of the crucifixion: the crown of thorns, the hammer, the nails, the sponge. These are all placed on a cushion on the ground. Viridiana, clad in a nightgown, is crouched in front of these things praying.

Interior of a stable, daytime. Close-up of the udder of a cow and the hand of the man who is milking it. It is the servant whom we have already seen as the coachman. Little Rita is perched on the wooden partition to which the cow is tied. Viridiana, carrying a basket, joins the group.

VIRIDIANA: Good morning. *(The servant answers politely.)* Good morning, Rita. How are we today?

RITA: Today a good girl.

VIRIDIANA *(to the servant):* Could I trouble you for my glass of milk?

SERVANT: Certainly, miss.

She takes a glass out of her basket and hands it to the servant. The man fills the glass straight from the udder. Viridiana watches him with curiosity.

VIRIDIANA: Is that difficult?

He looks at her for a moment as if he does not understand how anybody could ask him such a silly question.

SERVANT: Here, try it yourself.

The suggestion amuses Viridiana, but she declines.

VIRIDIANA: But I wouldn't know how.

He insists.

SERVANT: I'll show you. Hold here.

He grasps a teat and motions Viridiana to take it. Hesitating, she finally does so timidly. She sits on the stool that the servant pushes toward her. She blushes. She begins pulling the teat. Rita watches her clumsiness with contempt.

Viridiana obviously finds the sensation of the teat in her hand unpleasant. When no milk comes the servant insists, guiding her hand.

SERVANT: Pull hard like that and squeeze.

But Viridiana gives up the struggle with a gesture of disgust.

VIRIDIANA: I can't. It makes me... *(The servant looks at her without understanding.)* It makes me feel...

She trails off and goes to Rita. At the end of the stable the other servant, old Moncho, is carrying straw.

RITA: I saw you in your nightgown!

Viridiana looks at her angrily.

VIRIDIANA: What?

RITA: Yes, yes, I saw you!

MONCHO: Don't take her seriously, she's a liar.

The little girl turns to the old man furiously.

RITA: I saw her! I saw her... When she was dressing, her pins fell out and she picked them up.

Viridiana knows this is true. She takes Rita by the arm and speaks to her seriously.

VIRIDIANA: How did you see me?

RITA: From the terrace.

VIRIDIANA: It's very wicked to spy. Why did you do it? *(Moncho, shocked, bows his head resignedly. Viridiana smiles and addresses the little girl.)* I'm going to the hen house. Are you coming with me?

RITA: No, I don't want to.

Rita sulkily comes down from her perch and goes away. Viridiana thanks the servant, who hands her the glass of milk which she drinks.

Interior of the hen house. Viridiana takes the eggs that she finds in the nests and puts them in her basket.

DON JAIME'S VOICE: Hello!

There is a pause; Viridiana stops collecting the eggs.

VIRIDIANA: Good morning, Uncle. You're very early this morning.

DON JAIME *(off)*: So that I can see a little bit more of you.

The camera moves around the scene. The house is filled with egg crates and pigeons' nests. The pigeons fly in and out beneath the stone arcades.

VIRIDIANA: I'm going to make you a nun's cake. It will make your mouth water.

DON JAIME: You are spoiling me too much. I won't know what to do with myself when you've gone.

VIRIDIANA *(deliberately)*: Only because you want it.

Don Jaime walks up and down.

DON JAIME: What do you mean?

VIRIDIANA: Nothing. I didn't say anything.

A silence.

DON JAIME: You don't trust me, do you? What do you want to know?

She hesitates for a moment.

VIRIDIANA: Very well! I'm talking to you like this because I can't keep things to myself. *(She goes up to him and looks him straight in the eye.)* Is it true that you have a son?

Don Jaime is left momentarily speechless. He blushes.

DON JAIME: How did you know about that?

VIRIDIANA: Oh, some years ago I heard my mother talking about it. But is it true?

DON JAIME: Yes, it is.

VIRIDIANA: Don't you ever see him?

DON JAIME: Never.

VIRIDIANA: How could anybody behave like that?

DON JAIME: Sometimes these things happen because of inexperience. Sometimes it's because of...

VIRIDIANA *(interrupting)* : Evil.

DON JAIME: And what do you know about life? When all is said and done you couldn't possibly understand.

He walks forward a few steps looking worried.

VIRIDIANA: I understand perfectly. But even if you were not entirely blameworthy, you should have brought up the child.

Viridiana's expression becomes harder. Don Jaime begins to pace again nervously. He passes in front of his niece, speaking with a certain embarrassment.

Near by is a basin of water. While they are speaking Don Jaime looks down into the basin, on the edge of which a bee has settled.

DON JAIME: His mother wanted to keep him. She came from a poor family. I was in love with your aunt. I would like to have acknowledged him but I was afraid of losing her. That's why I didn't say anything.

VIRIDIANA: And this innocent child.

DON JAIME: Don't worry. He won't be forgotten.

There is silence. Viridiana picks up her basket again. Don Jaime stares obstinately at the basin. The bee is still there.

DON JAIME: You must think I am a monster.

VIRIDIANA: No, but what a pity life is like that.

The bee falls into the water. It flounders there, beating its legs and wings. Don Jaime puts a bit of bamboo into the water and lets the bee climb onto it.

DON JAIME: The poor little beast. It was going to drown.

Interior of the sitting room. It is two o'clock in the morning. The chimes dominate the music of the phonograph which plays a muted Ninth Symphony (fourth movement). The clock then strikes two.

The sitting room is lit only by the cheerful light of the wood burning in the hearth. Don Jaime's bedroom, opening off the end of the sitting room and lit by an oil lamp, appears to be empty. The camera pulls us into this room.

Interior of Don Jaime's room. Don Jaime is sitting in front of a large carved wooden chest which he has just opened. He seems to be concentrating but his expression is impassive. He is looking at the wedding attire he has kept, and judging from the cut of the clothes, they are the ones his dead wife Doña Elvira wore on her wedding day. Don Jaime gradually takes out the different parts of the outfit. He gazes at some of them for a moment; others he hardly looks at at all. There is the veil, the bodice, the skirt, the crown of artificial orange blossoms, the satin slippers.

He looks at some of these voluptuously. He throws the crown of orange blossoms onto his bed. He takes off his shoes and tries to put his bare foot into one of the delicate feminine slippers. Now he takes a satin corset with ribbons out of the chest. The chorus of the Ninth Symphony is still heard. With difficulty Don Jaime gets up and, with the corset in his hands, goes toward his mirror. He draws on the corset and gazes at his face.

Don Jaime's head and shoulders are reflected in the glass. His expression is blank. The music continues.

The log fire in the fireplace makes leaping shadows on the walls.

As Don Jaime is standing in front of the mirror a sudden noise makes him start. He rapidly hides the corset which he had wrapped around him and goes to the door.

DON JAIME *(in a broken voice)*: Who's there?

He hears the sound of furniture being knocked against. He sees Viridiana

pass two steps in front of him. She is barefoot. She has thrown over her nightgown a large woolen shawl which covers her shoulders. The girl does not seem to notice her uncle watching her and she continues to move toward the door of the sitting room. Crossing his room simultaneously, Don Jaime goes into the sitting room by the door which joins the two rooms.

The sitting room. Viridiana is carrying a wicker workbasket. Her eyes are

open but the expression on her face is cold, distant, statuesque. She goes directly to one of the armchairs near the fireplace and sits down.

Don Jaime comes into the sitting room. He follows the girl's movements with a dismayed look. He goes and stands in front of her. He sees that Viridiana is sleepwalking. He makes every effort to avoid making a noise but never takes his eyes off her.

As *Viridiana sits down her nightgown is disarranged and her leg and the beginning of her thigh are uncovered. Don Jaime stares at the white, finely grained flesh, unable to look away. He is visibly agitated.*

Viridiana takes the things that are in the workbasket — needles, balls of wool, skeins, and so on — and throws them into the fire. But her eyes do not see what her hands are doing. The precision of her movements is admirable; but as she makes another movement to draw nearer the fire, more of her thigh is exposed.

Don Jaime sadly closes his eyes. What a torment, to have so near his grasp the young woman he wishes to possess and yet dares not take in his arms!

He opens his eyes again. Apparently what he sees gives him an idea. But for the moment he is worried about what the young novice is doing.

Viridiana, kneeling now in front of the fire, takes handfuls of ashes and sprinkles them into her basket. Then she gets up and walks slowly toward Don Jaime's room and goes in. After a moment of astonished hesitation he follows her. As Viridiana reaches the bed, she empties the ashes from her basket, with a slow movement, onto the bedspread beside the orange blossoms Don Jaime threw there.

Don Jaime is startled; the expression on his face, seen in close-up, shows horror at the girl's apparently absurd conduct.

Viridiana walks back across the room. As she passes Don Jaime, the basket

in her hand brushes against him. Her eyes, still open, have a dead look in them, and since she is barefoot and walks slowly she seems to glide rather than walk. She leaves the room. Don Jaime goes to the bed and looks, in a distracted and incredulous way, at the ashes she has left there.

The hall. Viridiana walks toward her room. Don Jaime stands in the door-way of his bedroom watching his niece until she disappears into Doña Elvira's room.

The door of Doña Elvira's room closes very slowly. A faint click is heard as it is locked from the inside.

Interior of Don Jaime's room. Through the window which opens onto the balcony, the trees of the drive are seen standing out against the bright daytime sky.

Ramona is busy brushing a suit.

DON JAIME'S VOICE: Is she up yet?

RAMONA: She's been up for some time. *(She looks toward the bed where doubtless her master is and speaks, watching to see what his reaction will be.)* She asked me to get her things ready.

Don Jaime is shown sitting on his bed eating breakfast. What the servant has just said makes him start.

DON JAIME: Her last day in this house! I'll never see her again if she leaves.

At the other end of the room Ramona is now dusting a shelf.

RAMONA: Why don't you ask her to stay on for a few days?

DON JAIME *(put out)*: I have asked her but she's ungrateful. Some-times I feel like hitting her. When I talk to her about the convent, she turns to stone. *(He is frowning and seems to be thinking of something important. Almost pleading.)* Ramona! *(She stops dusting and looks intently at her master. He taps the edge of the bed.)* Come here, Ramona. *(The servant lays down her duster and shyly goes over to the bed.)* Sit down, I'm going to need your help.

RAMONA: What's the matter?

She hesitates; he takes her hand, forcing her to sit down on the edge of the bed.

DON JAIME: Sit down, woman, sit down. *(He looks into her eyes gently.)* You like me, don't you?

RAMONA: I'd be really ungrateful, if I didn't like you, sir; you took me and my little girl in when I didn't know where to turn.

DON JAIME: Yes, yes, but there's no need to bring that up. How far are you prepared to help me?

RAMONA: Just say the word, sir, and I'll do anything.

Without a doubt there is something at the back of his mind but he wants to feel his way first.

DON JAIME: Why don't you speak to her, Ramona? Women are good at that sort of thing. Think of something that will make her stay a few more days. *(He again takes her hand and caresses it.)* You are kind, Ramona! Speak to her. I know I don't need to offer you anything, but, if you're successful in this, I'll not forget you or your little girl.

RAMONA: But sir, what can I say to her? And why should she pay any attention to what a servant tells her?

Don Jaime twists his hands anxiously.

DON JAIME: You're right, but we must do something.

He continues to think thoughts that he dare not express.

RAMONA: *You* must think what the best thing to do is, and I'll help you to my utmost.

Don Jaime looks at his servant enigmatically, then speaks, without seeming to attach much importance to what he says.

DON JAIME: Look in the cupboard. On the upper shelf there's a little blue bottle. There's no label on it. You'll find some white pills inside.

While Don Jaime is speaking the cupboard is shown in close-up, half-open. Among other articles there are some bottles on one of the shelves. Ramona fully opens the cupboard door and takes one of the bottles. She turns to Don Jaime.

RAMONA: This one, sir?

Don Jaime nods in affirmation.

DON JAIME: Yes, leave it there. Go on with what you were doing. I'll tell you what to do later.

Ramona goes out of the room. Don Jaime puts down his tray on the small breakfast table and gets out of bed. He is in pajamas. He puts on his slippers and goes to the window. He looks out at the drive.

In the park below Don Jaime's window, Rita is jumping rope. Viridiana is standing near by. She stops the little girl. They talk for a moment, then the girl takes the rope and they begin to jump together very skillfully.

Don Jaime is watching the scene with the same enigmatic look on his face that he had a moment before and his eyes are full of tenderness.

The drawing room, daytime. Close-up of a woman's hands peeling fruit. The peel unrolls in a long spiral. It is Viridiana who is executing this work of art. She puts the fruit on a saucer and carries it to Don Jaime, who is sitting beside the fireplace where a good fire is blazing. On the little round table there are the remains of a meal which is just ending.

Don Jaime, his back turned three-quarters to the fireplace, is cleaning his pipes. He abandons them to thank his niece for her kindness. He admires the spiral.

DON JAIME: I have never been able to do that. I'm too nervous.

Viridiana, her back to the camera and to her uncle, gazes at the fire, lost for a moment in thought. She then turns and goes to Don Jaime and raises her arms in a gesture of incomprehension.

VIRIDIANA: Why didn't you wake me?

Don Jaime is eating the fruit.

DON JAIME: They say it's dangerous.

Viridiana seems to be ashamed of her bout of sleepwalking. She reacts energetically. She is trying to dismiss the matter as unimportant.

VIRIDIANA: I don't believe it. A few years ago – the last time I walked in my sleep – they woke me up by slapping my face.

And you can see I'm still alive. *(Her face darkens.)* What
worries me is that I put ashes on your bed.

Don Jaime is busy munching a piece of fruit.

DON JAIME; Why? It's no more odd than anything else. People who
walk in their sleep don't know what they're doing.

Viridiana, worried, shakes her head in disagreement.

VIRIDIANA: No, Uncle; ashes mean penance and death.

DON JAIME *(laughing)*: Then it's penance for you who are going to
be a nun; and for me, who am old, it's death... *(Viridiana
sits down. Ramona, who has come into the room a second before,
serves a cup of coffee to Don Jaime.)* If you like, I will come
with you tomorrow to the village when you leave.

VIRIDIANA: Thank you, Uncle.

Don Jaime examines the pipe which he is filling.

DON JAIME: This evening we must do something special by way of
a farewell.

VIRIDIANA: Whatever you like.

Don Jaime offers a piece of fruit to his niece. She takes it.

DON JAIME *(trying to appear detached about it)*: I should like you to
do something for me. It's an innocent sort of thing but I'm
very set on it.

VIRIDIANA: Today I can refuse you nothing.

Don Jaime, surprised and happy, gets up and comes over to her.

DON JAIME: You'll do what I ask, then?

Viridiana, not at all alarmed, bites the fruit which her uncle has given her.

VIRIDIANA: Whatever you wish. I'm at your command.

*He looks at her with gratitude. At the same time he is sincerely modest and
shy.*

DON JAIME: No, wait... *(He smiles awkwardly.)* What a silly thing! It's quite difficult for me to tell you what it is.

He takes a mouthful of coffee and relights his pipe. He shakes his head as if he is sorry for himself.

The park at night. The façade of the house is lit by the moon. The windows of the only two rooms which show light stand out in the darkness. Slowly the light fades in the window of Doña Elvira's room as if someone is carrying the light away. A dog is heard barking.

The hall. Viridiana, who appears clothed in the wedding dress previously seen in Don Jaime's hands, leaves Doña Elvira's room. She is holding a lit candelabra in her hand. She advances as if walking to the altar. Although the situation is not to her liking, she is a little amused by it. Ramona helps by carrying her train. They move toward the sitting room.

The sitting room. Don Jaime looks toward the door as the radiantly beautiful Viridiana enters the room. His hand shakes; he is motionless for a second. Then he goes toward her, takes the candelabra from her, and gazes at her in admiration. Ramona lets go of the train and goes off the frame.

DON JAIME *(very tenderly)*: How strange you are! When I asked you to do this favor for me you refused. You seemed almost offended. And now, here you are, making me so very happy all of a sudden. Thank you, my child!

VIRIDIANA *(a bit oppressed)*: I don't like masquerading, but as you see I decided to give in to your whim.

Don Jaime frees the girl's hand; he looks bitter.

DON JAIME: It's not a masquerade, nor is it a whim. *(He is silent for a moment.)* I'm going to tell you something that few people know. *(He takes a few steps with his fists clenched, stops, and turns to her.)* Your aunt died of a heart attack, in my arms, on our wedding night, wearing that dress, and you look so like her...

As he speaks he goes to the table, on which he places the candelabra. His words have moved the girl. Don Jaime follows her with his eyes.

DON JAIME: You must think I'm mad.

VIRIDIANA: No, Uncle, and now I'm pleased to have been able to do this favor, because, although I didn't think so at first, you are really a good man.

Viridiana adjusts her veil. Don Jaime has gone to another table near which Ramona is hovering. He lights the spirit lamp under a samovar.

DON JAIME: If you only knew… When I was young I was full of idealism. I wanted to do something on a big scale for others, something to show my great love for humanity. But as soon as I tried to do something about it, I became afraid that I would be laughed at and I felt like a fool… and so I went back into my shell.

VIRIDIANA: Wasn't that cowardice?

DON JAIME: No, it isn't that, I can assure you. I wouldn't be afraid in the face of real danger. I've proved that to myself. On the other hand, if a stranger visited me simply to say hello, I'd be alarmed. *(There is silence for a moment. Don Jaime looks at Viridiana almost lovingly.)* I can't take my eyes off you. Come, let's sit down.

They sit side by side.

VIRIDIANA: Uncle, you musn't think that I won't be sad to leave you.

DON JAIME *(eagerly):* It's up to you entirely. Don't leave, then...

Viridiana shakes her head.

VIRIDIANA: Unfortunately...

DON JAIME *(discouraged):* It's my fault. If I'd come to see you more often, if I'd invited you here for holidays, maybe everything would be different.

VIRIDIANA *(smiling):* Maybe...

Don Jaime gazes at his niece. His tension is at a peak. His whole future depends on what he is about to say; he is convinced of that.

DON JAIME: There's one way you could stay. If I asked... *(He stops in front of her; he lowers his eyes.)* I mean... if I said to you... *(He cannot go on. His mouth is dry and he is flushed, his muscles contracting.)* No, I can't... I can't...

Viridiana looks at him in amazement.

Ramona comes up to them. The servant has followed the conversation with interest and anxiety. She comes to her master's assistance. She quickly intervenes to address the girl in a firm tone.

RAMONA: What he wants, miss, is to marry you. *(This remark leaves the girl stunned.)* Excuse me, sir, but I only said what you didn't dare say yourself. *(Don Jaime is ashamed and looks at the servant reproachfully.)* He loves you very much and he deserves to be loved in return, because he is a very good man.

Viridiana has not yet got over her surprise. Perhaps she is even more upset than he is. But gradually she frowns and shows her irritation.

VIRIDIANA: You're really serious?

Don Jaime answers her in a determined voice but with his eyes lowered.

DON JAIME: Yes, I don't want you ever to leave this house.

VIRIDIANA *(getting up)*: You must be out of your mind. I've been so happy these last few days – now you've spoiled it all. *(A silence. Viridiana pulls off her veil angrily.)* I think it would be better if I went to my room.

She moves toward the door. Don Jaime rushes forward to restrain her.

DON JAIME: Wait! Forgive me! Honestly, I really beg your pardon. Stay a few more minutes! If you go now, I'm afraid you'll always resent me. I promise not to say anything that might annoy you. I'll put some music on and we'll have a cup of coffee.

Don Jaime makes a sign to Ramona, who has gone over to the sideboard where the coffeepot is. Viridiana is motionless, her head hangs, she refuses to say a word. Ramona looks at Don Jaime, who signals to her almost imperceptibly. He goes to the phonograph and puts on a classical record, as usual. Viridiana, head still down, has just sat down in the armchair. Ramona fills the coffeecups. The phonograph begins to play.

RAMONA: Take this, miss, it'll do you good.

Ramona offers a cup of coffee to the girl. Gazing in front of her, she drinks almost the whole cup in a quick gulp.

The servants' quarters, nighttime. A very simple room on the ground floor of the house. An old sideboard and a rough kitchen table. Moncho is sitting near the table mending a strap. Beside him is a piece of paper with lumps of sugar on it. He eats them with enthusiasm, munching noisily. The door opens and little Rita comes in, sobbing and frightened. She is barefoot, dressed in a skirt and an old ragged blanket which covers the upper part of her body. The old servant looks at her disapprovingly.

MONCHO: Why are you crying?

RITA: I'm afraid.

MONCHO: Don't invent stories; go to bed.

RITA: A black bull came.

MONCHO *(laughing mockingly)* : A black bull!

Rita approaches him. Her fear is disappearing.

RITA: It's a very big one.

MONCHO: Very, very?

RITA *(with an air of defiance)* : Yes – very, very big!

MONCHO: He couldn't get through the door, then?

Rita shakes her head vigorously. Moncho laughs with an air of "Now you've been caught in a barefaced lie."

MONCHO: Then how did it get in, silly?

The little girl thinks for a moment.

RITA *(energetically)* : He came in through the cupboard.

MONCHO: You little liar! Get out of here!

Rita starts crying again.

RITA: I'm afraid.

Moncho holds out a piece of sugar to her.

MONCHO: Here! And call your mother if you're having nightmares. Now go away and don't annoy me.

Rita accepts the gifts and lingers for a moment. The servant carries on with his work and finally the girl leaves, munching her lump of sugar.

The sitting room. Ramona puts down her cup. Then Don Jaime gives her his. They look at each other in silence. The music has stopped. Don Jaime goes to the phonograph and switches it on again. Viridiana is still sitting, with her back to the camera, holding the empty cup in her hand. Don Jaime comes up behind her.

Close-up of Viridiana's right hand holding the cup and saucer. Her fingers slacken and she lets go of them. Don Jaime holds his breath. He is just behind her. He stops to watch her reactions. He looks at Ramona. Then he speaks.

DON JAIME *(in a shaky voice):* You look very tired. Perhaps you'd better go to bed.

There is no reply. Viridiana's head falls on her shoulders. Don Jaime comes toward her slowly until he is standing in front of her. He shakes her gently.

DON JAIME: Viridiana! Viridiana!...

There is no reply.

The hall. The only light comes from the sitting room. At the end of the hall, the small silhouette of Rita appears as she comes upstairs. She carefully enters the hall, going in the direction of the sitting room, from which muffled voices are heard.

DON JAIME'S VOICE: Help me... Take her by the legs.

RAMONA'S VOICE: Lift her a little more, sir...

A pause. There is the sound of a chair being overturned.

DON JAIME'S VOICE: Don't think too badly of me, Ramona; I only want to have her close to me.

The camera reaches Rita. There is the sound of footsteps approaching the door and the child runs and hides herself behind the staircase, from where, timorously, she watches the scene. Don Jaime and his servant appear from the sitting room, carrying Viridiana who appears to be dead. They go toward Doña Elvira's room and enter it. Rita comes out of her hiding place. Her curiosity aroused, she would like to see more but she is afraid of being discovered. She withdraws gradually and starts to go downstairs again.

Inside Doña Elvira's room. Don Jaime and Ramona have laid Viridiana motionless on the bed. Ramona lights the candles.

DON JAIME'S VOICE *(off)* : That will be all, Ramona.

She obeys in silence.

Viridiana remains lying on her back motionless. Her hair is slightly untidy, as it was a few minutes before in the sitting room. Don Jaime, feverishly,

with an artist's meticulousness, begins to perfect his masterpiece. He crosses the girl's arms over her breast, puts her feet together, arranges the pleats of her dress. Lying thus, Viridiana has the look of a lovely figure on a tomb.

The scene switches to the big tree which dominates the grounds. We see Rita going toward it, looking up from time to time at the feebly lit window of Doña Elvira's room. After a moment's hesitation, the little girl begins to climb the tree. As she ascends, the sound of a dog barking is heard in the night.

Doña Elvira's room. Don Jaime, sitting on the edge of the bed, stands up. For a moment he walks up and down in front of the motionless body, without taking his eyes off it. He stops for a second, then goes over and sits on the bed again. He caresses Viridiana's hair and forehead. He is terribly affected. Then he puts his arms around the girl's shoulders and lifts her gently into a sitting position. He draws his face close to hers and joins his lips to hers in a sweet, prolonged kiss.

The window, through which little Rita, who has reached the terrace, looks curiously in at the scene.

With trembling hands Don Jaime unfastens the neck of Viridiana's dress. Her throat and the top of her breasts are exposed. The body he has been yearning for, now defenseless, is at his mercy. He is completely beside himself. He lays his cheek against Viridiana's breast. He feels the softness of the skin and its warmth. He kisses it once, twice. Suddenly he reacts. He gets up with a start and looks, almost with terror, at the body. He sees the calm, serene expression on the girl's face. Don Jaime now passes from the realm of blind instinct to the realm of conscience. He realizes the meanness of his actions. Basically he is a good and kindly man. Nevertheless his hands reach out to her again. Then suddenly, decisively, as if moved by fear of himself, he runs to the door, opens it, and goes out into the hall, taking the lit candelabra with him on the way. The music has not stopped throughout.

Rita climbs down from the branches of the tree and jumps to the ground. She sees her mother waiting for her and runs to join her.

RAMONA: What are you doing?

RITA: Don Jaime was kissing the lady.

Ramona, with a somber look, stares at her child. Then she sees how Rita has come to know this. She frowns, annoyed.

RAMONA: He only kisses her because she's his niece. Don't I kiss you? You should be in bed.

RITA: A black bull came into my room.

RAMONA: Be quiet. I'm going to put you to bed.

She takes her by the hand and leads her to the servants' door.

Again the barking of a dog is heard.

Don Jaime passes down the hall on his way to his room, walking quickly and nervously. He opens the door, enters, and closes it with a bang. Absolute silence then reigns in the house.

Interior of Doña Elvira's room the next day. Ramona, standing in front of the window, closes it. We hear the moaning voice of Viridiana.

VIRIDIANA *(off)*: I'm thirsty.

Ramona gives her a glass of water from a bottle that is on the console. Viridiana drinks it greedily.

RAMONA: How do you feel?

VIRIDIANA: I have a headache.

RAMONA: That will soon pass. It's nothing.

Viridiana notices her exposed body and covers herself modestly – ill at ease.

VIRIDIANA: What happened to me?

RAMONA: You fainted last night after supper. The master and I
    carried you here.

VIRIDIANA: Have I slept long?

RAMONA: Oh, you slept well; don't worry.

The sound of footsteps is heard approaching the bedroom. Viridiana covers herself under the bedclothes. The door opens and Don Jaime appears. His face and the untidiness of his clothes show clearly that he must have spent a sleepless night. Seeing him, Viridiana wants to protest but does not dare. Don Jaime comes in.

DON JAIME: Leave us alone, Ramona.

VIRIDIANA *(vehemently)*: Don't go!

Don Jaime makes a sign with his head and the servant obeys. She leaves the room, closing the door behind her. The uncle and niece remain, facing one another.

VIRIDIANA: Leave me alone, uncle, please. I want to get up.

She receives no reply. The old man walks up and down the room, deep in thought, obviously not knowing how to begin. She insists, in an irritated manner.

VIRIDIANA: I have to go!

Don Jaime sits down on the edge of the bed. He answers very decisively.

DON JAIME: No. You can never go away now.

There is a sudden look of impatience, almost of real fear, in the girl's eyes.

VIRIDIANA: Last night you promised never to speak of that again. I beg you, leave me alone.

The old man does not budge.

DON JAIME: What could be more unlike than an old man who lives alone and a young woman like you, consecrated to God. However...

The girl, exasperated, almost sits up in bed.

VIRIDIANA *(violently)* : Be quiet! I don't want to listen to you! Don't you understand that I want to get dressed?

He, lost in thought, does not seem to hear her.

DON JAIME: I forgot everything because of you, even the passion that has kept me going all these years... everything.

He gets up and walks around the room. Viridiana would like to get up and force him to leave the room, but her state of semi-nudity prevents her.

DON JAIME: I must have been mad. I thought that you would agree to marry me, but naturally you refused. And now it's the day that you must leave.

She looks at him, wondering how the discussion is going to end. Don Jaime comes to the bed and leans over her. He stares at her.

DON JAIME *(coldly)*: I had to force you. *(Pause.)* That was the only way I could find to have you in my arms.

Viridiana evidences growing dismay and anxiety.

VIRIDIANA *(shouting)*: You're lying.

DON JAIME: No, it's true. *(Speaking each word distinctly.)* Last night when you were sleeping, I had you all to myself.

She opens her eyes wide in horror. She can't believe what he's saying. She feels a cold sweat breaking out on her forehead. Don Jaime starts pacing back and forth again in front of her, sometimes staring at her and sometimes obstinately lowering his eyes.

DON JAIME: Now you won't be able to go back to your convent. You're not the same woman who left it a few days ago. Now, you'll have to stay with me here forever.

He stops, comes back to the bed, and sits down. There is a pleading note in his voice.

DON JAIME: Everything I have will be yours, and if you don't want to marry me, if you prefer to live as we have up to now, provided you're close to me, I'll content myself with...

She visibly takes time to understand her uncle's words. The blow is so hard that she hardly even reacts. Her plight moves Don Jaime to sympathy.

DON JAIME: Think about it. Don't hurry. Think it over.

VIRIDIANA *(with a start, almost shouting)*: Go away! Leave me alone.

She looks at him with hate and disgust. Don Jaime is affected. He hesitates. He starts to speak to her again but does not do so. He finally gets up and goes to the door. He feels Viridiana's eyes, blazing with anger, upon him. He leaves the room, head hanging, shattered. Immediately Viridiana leaps out of bed, grabs her bag, and wildly begins to throw her clothes into it.

At the door of Don Jaime's room Ramona is waiting for Don Jaime, whom we see coming from the hall. He passes the servant without noticing her. He goes into the room. Ramona goes up to him slowly.

RAMONA: What did you say to her, sir?

He looks at her.

DON JAIME: The way she looked at me, Ramona! She hates me now. I think I've made a great mistake. She's going away, she's going away and nothing will stop her.

RAMONA *(without conviction)*: Speak to her again. Explain everything to her seriously.

DON JAIME: What for? She'll only look at me that way again... I couldn't. You go. Perhaps she'll listen to you. Try to convince her.

RAMONA: But what can I say to her, sir?

DON JAIME: Tell her I lied, that I didn't take advantage of her. *(Ramona looks at him, stunned, incredulous. He continues with sincerity.)* I did mean to do it, Ramona. But I realized in time what I was doing. I spent the whole night turning my thoughts over in my mind... and I lied to her so she wouldn't go back to the convent. *(Taking Ramona by the arm.)* Go on, explain to her.

He almost pushes her to the door. She goes against her will, hesitating. He watches her from the doorway.

In Doña Elvira's room. Viridiana has dressed and is closing her bag. Ramona comes in stealthily through the half-open door. Viridiana's eyes are full of tears. In the background Ramona hesitates for a moment, then half turns and goes back quickly to Don Jaime's room.

In his room Don Jaime is leaning against the bed. Ramona appears in the doorway.

RAMONA: Sir, come right away.

Don Jaime straightens himself with a start. He stares at the servant for a second. Then he walks quickly to the door and goes out.

Doña Elvira's room. Viridiana grabs her bag and is just about to go as her uncle enters. He blocks her way and locks the door, taking the key from the lock. The girl still has signs of tears on her face.

VIRIDIANA: Let me pass!

DON JAIME: You must listen to me before you go.

VIRIDIANA *(angrily)*: I've listened to you long enough. Let me out.

Viridiana goes back a couple of steps and puts down her bag. She is no longer afraid. She can hardly feel any emotion except anger mingled with disgust. Don Jaime remains standing beside her.

DON JAIME: All that I said just now was a lie. I said it so you wouldn't leave. I only molested you in my thoughts... I can't bear to have you leave me, hating me like this. *(Pleadingly.)* Tell me you believe what I'm saying and I'll let you go.

VIRIDIANA: You disgust me... even if what you say is true.

DON JAIME *(in a quieter voice)*: Then you won't forgive me?

The young woman's look shatters Don Jaime. With difficulty, Viridiana, who has turned her back to her uncle, holds back the sobs which are choking her. After a moment's anguished silence, Don Jaime, resigned to his fate, holds the key out to the girl. She snatches it from him, takes up her suitcase, and makes for the door; she goes out without a glance in his direction.

As Viridiana comes out of Doña Elvira's room into the hall, Ramona is seen walking toward her away from the camera. Don Jaime's silhouette hovers on the threshold which the girl has just crossed. Viridiana passes in front of the camera and her rushing footsteps are heard descending the staircase.

Doña Elvira's room. Don Jaime is looking out from the balcony. Ramona enters, shaken by all that has happened. Hearing her footsteps, Don Jaime turns around. His expression is not what one would expect. He seems calm, without the slightest trace of disappointment. He seems even to be smiling. Now that what he has feared so much has occurred, he is recovering his former courage. The servant stops a few feet away, her eyes lowered, not daring to look at him. Don Jaime goes to her.

DON JAIME: You believe me, don't you?

RAMONA: Yes, sir.

Her voice is low, utterly without conviction. Don Jaime notices this. He smiles.

DON JAIME: Don't lie. You don't believe me either.

RAMONA *(trying to find an excuse)*: It's only that... It's all very odd, sir.

Don Jaime nods his head sympathetically.

DON JAIME: It's all right, my girl, it's all right.

He makes for the hall. Ramona goes to the unmade bed and examines the sheets, as if trying to discover the truth. Seeing nothing, she sits on the edge of the bed with a thoughtful air.

In the park the coachman finishes preparing the carriage. Some yards away Viridiana is waiting, seated on a stone bench with her back to the camera. Her bag is at her side. Near by Rita is playing diabolo. The toys Don Jaime gives her indicate how old-fashioned he is.

RITA: See how high I can throw it!

Viridiana does not even look around. In order to attract her attention, Rita collects the spool which has fallen back onto the string. She turns it and puts it into place with the aid of one of the sticks.

RITA: Look! *You* can't do that!

As Viridiana remains sunk deep in thought, Rita loses heart and tries to interest Moncho, who has just picked up Viridiana's bag and is taking it to the carriage.

RITA: Look! Moncho! Look how high it is!

As usual, he answers her in a surly manner.

MONCHO: Let me have a little peace, won't you?

Rita goes on playing without paying any attention to his bad temper. Moncho approaches Viridiana.

MONCHO: When you're ready, miss.

The girl stands up and goes to the carriage.

The balcony outside Don Jaime's room. Don Jaime watches his niece's departure. As Viridiana goes to the carriage Rita says something to her, but she merely caresses her head with her hand as a sign of farewell. She gets in and the coachman gives the horse the whip. The little girl waves goodbye, then begins to run after the carriage.

Don Jaime sadly watches the carriage disappear. But he recovers quickly and his face takes on a calm, almost indifferent look. He goes to the desk which is in the corner of the room and sits down at it. He rubs his forehead. The writing materials on the table are lying in disorder. Several months must certainly have passed since he has been near his desk. Carefully he begins to make order out of the chaos. He rubs his fingers along the table to see if there is any dust on it. Seeing that it is clean, he smiles at the thought of Ramona's conscientiousness. Finally he takes a pen and a sheet of notepaper and begins to write. He smiles quietly, rubbing his beard dreamily. He appears to have thought of something that pleases him very much.

The village square. Under the arcade which borders the square, Viridiana is waiting for her bus to arrive; its approach is heralded by the sound of its engine. She goes to the bus stop, where others are waiting. As the bus stops, passengers get off and those who were waiting get on. The driver comes up to Viridiana.

DRIVER: I'll take your bag, please, miss.

At this moment an important-looking middle-class gentleman comes along the arcade, followed by two uniformed policemen and a peasant. The group comes up to Viridiana, to whom the man holds out his hand.

GENTLEMAN: How do you do, Miss Viridiana!

VIRIDIANA: Is anything the matter, Mr. Mayor?

MAYOR: You cannot leave...

VIRIDIANA *(surprised)*: Why not?

MAYOR: There's been an accident.

VIRIDIANA: Where?

MAYOR: Come with me.

He takes her by the arm. Viridiana neither protests nor asks any further questions.

Don Jaime's estate. A car stops in the drive. The mayor gets out, followed by the group which was with him in the village. All come toward the camera, eyes trained on the branches of the big tree beside which Rita likes to play. Moncho rushes up to meet them.

Near the tree, Ramona and her daughter, clinging to one another watch the people arrive.

The big tree, through whose foliage hang the feet of a man.

Close-up of Viridiana, who has just got out of the car and sees the body. Overcome, she leans her forehead against the car door and remains like that for a moment, motionless and silent.

Close-up of the branch from which Don Jaime is hanging. The only part of him that is visible is the back of his head. The body itself is outside the frame. The rope which is tied to the branch has a wooden handle. It is Rita's jump-rope.

The turrets of the house and the trees of the park.

The same picture of little Rita's legs skipping under the big tree as at the beginning of the film.

Moncho, who is leading a horse, stops upon seeing Rita. He lets go of the animal's halter and goes up to the little girl. Brutally he takes hold of the jumprope and tries to snatch it from her. Rita struggles with him fiercely.

RITA: Give it to me. It's mine!

The old man elbows her aside.

MONCHO: I'll box your ears if you don't show some respect for the dead! You mustn't play under this tree.

RITA: Don Jaime loved to watch me skip.

The servant finally seizes the rope and throws it away.

MONCHO: If something terrible happens now it will be your fault.

He leaves. As soon as his back is turned, Rita picks up the rope and with the same liveliness begins to skip. The picture of her legs again.

Viridiana's room. Close-up of her black wooden cross and the crown of thorns hooked across the end of the bed. The room has a red brick floor and whitewashed walls.

Viridiana, who undoubtedly did not want to keep the room she was in before, is now in a less elaborate room on the ground floor. The furniture consists of an iron bed, two chairs, and a white wooden table. In the corner there is a very simple dressing-table without a mirror. Viridiana, with bucket and broom, is washing the floor. The young woman's face is more drawn and she is no longer smiling. Something seems to have happened to her: she appears youthful, and with a certain balance that she lacked before.

Ramona comes into the room and puts a tray on the table. She lifts off the napkin, revealing the meal of a plate of vegetables, a glass of milk, and a piece of bread.

RAMONA: You aren't eating enough. I've given you a glass of milk, and this evening I'll bring you some meat. *(Viridiana stops working and goes to wash her hands in a basin on the dressing-table.)* You don't look at all well! *(Viridiana does not answer.)* The mayor told me that he's dealing with the problems you were talking about. You can go to the village when you want to. It'll do you good to see the world.

In the distance a car is heard: it stops. Ramona looks out the open window...

Two nuns pass outside and into the building. One of them is the Mother Superior of Viridiana's convent.

Viridiana goes to the door. Unruffled, she watches the Mother Superior enter. Ramona moves back to let the visitor pass and then leaves the room.

MOTHER SUPERIOR: Good morning. You weren't expecting me, were you?

VIRIDIANA: Mother.

The Mother Superior looks at Viridiana with compassion. She shakes her head with pity.

MOTHER SUPERIOR: You must have suffered, my child!

The young girl goes up to her, but instead of throwing herself into her arms weeping, as her Superior seems to expect, she bows deeply and calmly kisses the crucifix on the Mother Superior's rosary. This calm somewhat disconcerts her visitor.

MOTHER SUPERIOR: Ever since yesterday, when we heard by chance about the tragedy, we have been very anxious for you. Why didn't you write? I would have come immediately.

VIRIDIANA: I had so many things to think about!

MOTHER SUPERIOR: A suicide is horrible. I know. But you should have told me. *(She looks around her and seems to approve of the simplicity of the room.)* I talked for a few minutes to the parish priest in the village and he told me how it happened. Everybody is asking why this horrible offense was committed against Our Lord. Do you know the reason?

Viridiana remains standing.

VIRIDIANA: I only know that my uncle was a grave sinner and I feel guilty for his death.

The Mother Superior's face darkens. She moves toward Viridiana.

MOTHER SUPERIOR: How can you say that? You, responsible for the suicide of a man? I want a complete confession from you.

Viridiana lowers her eyes.

VIRIDIANA *(firmly)* : I'm not going back to the convent; therefore I'm no longer under obedience to anyone.

She says this calmly, almost humbly, but there is an element of revolt in her voice which angers her Superior, who struggles to control herself. The Superior swallows hard and speaks without raising her voice.

MOTHER SUPERIOR : Is there some grave impediment which prevents you from taking your vows? There must be something.

VIRIDIANA : I have nothing to reproach myself for. All I know is that I've changed. With all my strength, which is not much,

I will follow the road that the Lord has shown me. One can also serve outside a convent.

MOTHER SUPERIOR: Are you aware of the pride there is in what you're saying?

Viridiana does not answer. She continues to look down. The nun changes her tone. She tries irony.

MOTHER SUPERIOR: What great plans are you thinking of dedicating yourself to now?

Viridiana looks her in the eye.

VIRIDIANA: I know my own weakness, and whatever I do will be humble. But however little it is I want to do it alone.

There is a moment of silence while the Mother Superior tries to follow Viridiana's train of thought. Her amazement prevails over her indignation. She does not know what to think. Finally she speaks, very dryly.

MOTHER SUPERIOR: Very well. As you won't let me help you, I must leave you. I'm very sorry I came and disturbed you. Goodbye.

She half turns and goes to the door.

VIRIDIANA: Mother! *(The Mother Superior stops.)* Forgive me if I have offended you.

MOTHER SUPERIOR: You are forgiven. Goodbye.

She goes out, closing the door behind her.

The Church square of the village, flooded with sunlight. A little old man dressed in rags half walks, half runs, up to a group of beggars as shabbily dressed as himself who are standing in the doorway of the church. The beggars are Don Amalio, blind, about 45; El Pelón (Baldy), a rather alarming character of about 40; Enedina, who is carrying a two-year-old girl in her arms; Refugio, a woman of uncertain age, showing obvious signs of pregnancy; and finally, the little old man who has just arrived and who answers to the nickname "El Poca".

Don Amalio, who has the hard, sharp features of a countryman is sitting with his back against the stone steps of the church, his face absorbing the sun. Near him lies a long white stick which acts as a guide when he walks. In his arms he holds Enedina's second little girl, who is about a year old. As people pass him on their way into the church, he calls out sonorously for alms.

PELÓN: Why isn't she coming?

POCA: She has already crossed herself.

REFUGIO: She's a very firm believer.

There is a silence. Some of them look toward the church door.

ENEDINA: I've heard she's even going to pay us to go and live with her.

Two women pass.

DON AMALIO: Kind people! Don't forget a poor blind man.

In the background Viridiana comes out of the church. The beggars are in confusion. Poca grasps the blind man by the arm and pulls him to his feet.

POCA: There she is. Hurry up, come on. You've had it if you totter around like that and fool with the kids.

Viridiana joins them. She takes the child from Amalio.

VIRIDIANA: Give the little girl to me. Come here, sweetheart. Are you ready?

PELÓN: When you are, miss.

VIRIDIANA: Good, then let's go!

Poca, who is leading the old man, comes up to Viridiana. He looks at her and speaks to Don Amalio.

POCA: She has the face of an angel. What a pity you can't see her.

VIRIDIANA: Right, let's go. *(To Poca.)* And keep the compliments to yourself. I don't like them.

The beggars get their belongings together, then join up.

In another little square of the village two more beggars are waiting : one is Don Zequiel, an old man of about sixty whose full white beard gives him the look of a patriarch ; the other is a man of about forty, with a black beard. He moves with the help of a stick and is known by the name of Hobbly. He is drinking from the fountain of the small square when the group led by Viridiana comes toward them.

DON ZEQUIEL: Here they come.

Hobbly turns away from the fountain to look at them.

VIRIDIANA: Are you the other two?

DON ZEQUIEL: Yes, miss, that's us, yes.

VIRIDIANA: Good, come with me.

Interior of Don Jaime's sitting room. Close-up of an oil portrait of Don Jaime.

JORGE'S VOICE *(off)*: What a strange man! I wish I knew what he was like.

LUCIA'S VOICE *(off)*: As far as you're concerned, worthless. You can see how much he cared about you.

The people who are speaking come into view. Jorge, Don Jaime's son, no more than thirty, is a well-built energetic type. Not overimaginative or a dreamer, he is a practical man of action. His custom-made clothes look recently cleaned and pressed. Lucia is younger. She is pretty and pleasant but there is nothing to distinguish her from many other women. She too seems dressed in her Sunday best.

JORGE: I'm not at all bitter about it. Anyone can love and forget. But... Why did he acknowledge me at the last moment? What was going through his mind?

Ramona, who is coming out of Don Jaime's room, is listening. She looks at the portrait tenderly.

RAMONA: He was very good. Better than some people would think.

JORGE: Why did he kill himself?

Ramona tries not to show anything of what she knows, or her sorrow.

RAMONA: I don't know, sir.

JORGE *(nodding)*: One shouldn't be alone the whole time. *(He looks at Lucia; laughing.)* I'm not like him, am I?

He goes to the harmonium. Lucia follows him.

LUCIA: Not in that way; you're always looking for company.

JORGE: Why do you say that?

Perhaps the young girl is a bit jealous.

LUCIA *(off)*: I know what I mean.

Jorge pedals the harmonium and runs his hands across the keyboard, causing a series of discords. Ramona cannot bear this profanation and interrupts.

RAMONA: Don't play, sir.

He takes his hands from the keyboard and looks at the servant in astonishment.

RAMONA *(respectfully)*: I beg your pardon, sir. The master used to play here by the hour. It was a real delight to listen to him.

She closes the harmonium slowly. Jorge leans against the instrument and stares at her, looking half the seducer and half ironic. The servant, disturbed, slips away.

RAMONA: If you don't mind, I'll go get the other suitcase.

Lucia, looking sulky, goes past them onto the balcony. Jorge follows her.

The balcony looks out on a wasteland: scorched terrain, with some scrub and weeds; some trees and among them some dilapidated outhouses of the old farm. There are mountains in the background.

JORGE: Look at these beautiful fields! And behind those pines the fields, dried up and abandoned. There's so much to do here and it's all mine. We won't have time to get bored.

Lucia smiles. Jorge takes the young girl by the shoulders and draws her to him. He wants to embrace her, but she pulls away.

JORGE: Aren't you happy?

She seems rather sad, in fact.

LUCIA: Yes. But I don't know... I wish I hadn't come.

Obviously her lover is everything to her, but she fears that this unexpected prosperity might separate them. Something happening in the drive attracts Lucia's attention and she points.

LUCIA: Look at that.

Jorge leans over the balcony and looks at what is happening below.

The park. Viridiana is coming into the park followed by her troup of beggars. The beggars, in little groups, are looking around with curiosity. Poca and the blind man Don Amalio are among them. Poca is telling the blind man what he sees.

POCA *(full of admiration for the house)* : It's very big...

The blind man hits the ground with his stick.

DON AMALIO: So much the better. We'll all fit. How many floors are there?

POCA: Two.

DON AMALIO: Are there many windows?

POCA: Lots. It's got balconies and two big towers.

DON AMALIO *(sententiously)* : Then it's a respectable house.

The old servant Moncho comes out of the house and approaches the arrivals.

VIRIDIANA: Have you repaired the windows of the dormitories?

MONCHO: They shut all right now. And the blankets are ready.

Enedina and Refugio bring up the end of the line.

REFUGIO: That miss is as good as gold.

ENEDINA: She's very good, but a bit of a simpleton.

The group stops near the house.

VIRIDIANA: The men will sleep on one side, the women on the

other, but we will eat together. We'll try to get you some decent clothes tomorrow. Moncho, show them where they'll be. I'll take the women.

Jorge and Lucia have come out of the house and are looking with curiosity and astonishment at this tattered group. They go up to Viridiana.

JORGE: Viridiana. *(Viridiana turns and notices the couple without showing any surprise. Jorge bows.)* Miss Viridiana...

VIRIDIANA: Are you Jorge?

She shakes the hand he is stretching out.

JORGE: Jorge, Don Jaime's son, at your service.

VIRIDIANA: I've been expecting you; I got a letter from the lawyer.

She looks at Lucia.

JORGE *(smiling)*: This is Lucia; she's a good girl. You'll get to know each other very quickly.

They shake hands.

Little Rita has come out of the house and rushes toward the beggars, brushing past Lucia. The beggars are waiting near the house. Moncho goes through them to get in front. Old Don Zequiel paternally puts his hand on Rita's head.

DON ZEQUIEL: What's your name?

RITA *(lively)*: Don't touch me! You're going to sleep in the farmyard with the chickens!

Moncho gestures to the men to follow him.

MONCHO: Get moving! Anyone who pokes around where he shouldn't be will pay for it.

They begin walking, but the blind man is offended by these words.

DON AMALIO: Listen, although we may be poor, every man has his dignity, brother.

MONCHO: Don't "brother" me: there aren't any scum in my family.

Pelón, who doesn't inspire sympathy, understands the allusion.

PELÓN: Well now, even the servants put on airs here, don't they?

Moncho stops and turns around.

MONCHO *(angrily)* : Do you want me to smash your face?

Viridiana, who is following with the women, hears this exchange and goes up to the beggars.

VIRIDIANA: What's going on, Moncho?

MONCHO: This louse is looking for trouble.

Pelón hardly lets him finish.

PELÓN: You runt.

Moncho is about to attack but Viridiana stops him.

VIRIDIANA *(to Pelón)* : Don't talk like that!

PELÓN: I'll talk the way I want to. I've had enough of this.

The blind man, guided by the voices, is angered by Pelón's lack of respect and hits him with his stick.

DON AMALIO: That'll teach you some manners.

PELÓN: Blind, shit! You can see now.

He attacks Don Amalio. All of them intervene to separate the two. Viridiana fearlessly stands between them.

VIRIDIANA *(shouting with authority)* : In you go! Moncho, lead the way! *(To Pelón.)* You stay here.

MONCHO: But, miss...

Jorge and Lucia are anxiously watching the absurd proceedings. Jorge is about to intervene but Lucia stops him.

LUCIA: Leave her.

The beggars, both men and women, are calmer. The blind man is muttering. Pelón looks at Viridiana venomously.

VIRIDIANA: Keep calm, Moncho. And you *(to the blind man)*, don't be quarrelsome!

Moncho, unwillingly resigning himself to the situation, goes forward followed by the beggars. Viridiana calmly goes up to Pelón.

VIRIDIANA: Would you mind telling me what I did wrong to you to deserve your insults?

PELÓN: I've had a gutful of this.

VIRIDIANA: If you want to stay you'll have to exercise a little self-control, and be a bit more humble to everybody.

The beggar shrugs his shoulders contemptuously.

PELÓN: If that's the way, it's better to leave. *(He half turns and walks away a few steps, but then he hesitates a moment and turns around again, facing the young woman.)* Give me something to go on with. *(Viridiana reaches in her pocket and gives Pelón some money.)* Because we are poor, without it...

He leaves. In the background, Jorge and Lucia go back into the house.

The beggars split up into two groups. On the left the men are led by Moncho and on the right are the women; Viridiana joins them.

The sitting room at night. Close-up of a basin of hot water which is still steaming. In the water are the feet of Jorge, who has rolled up his trousers. He is dressed for the country. He is sitting on Don Jaime's special armchair and smoking one of his pipes. Lucia, sitting on a small low chair in front of him, has just finished polishing his boots. They are silent. She looks at him now and then.

LUCIA *(off)*: Are you tired?

JORGE: I nearly walked my legs off today. *(He rubs his legs. Pointing to the basin.)* That has done me good.

There is a silence. Ramona comes in with a towel in her hand. She hands it to Jorge and then looks at Lucia, who goes on wiping the boots which have been waxed.

RAMONA: Why don't you let me do that, miss?

LUCIA *(dryly)*: Because I've got him into bad habits.

Jorge begins to dry his feet. The maid bends down to pick up the basin, gets up, and turns. She goes to the door but stops before going out.

RAMONA: Whenever you're ready I can serve supper.

LUCIA: Right, we'll have it now.

The maid leaves the room after glancing at the little table which is already laid. Jorge, suddenly in a bad mood, flings his towel to the floor. Lucia looks at him in surprise.

LUCIA *(harshly)*: What's the matter with you?

JORGE: Nothing.

LUCIA: Why the bad temper?

JORGE: It's Viridiana. She's getting on my nerves.

Lucia has finished his shoes and puts them in a corner.

LUCIA *(shrugging)*: She's mad.

JORGE: No, not mad at all: she's rotten with religion.

LUCIA: Let her do what she wants. She doesn't bother us in any way. She minds her business and we... *(They fall silent. Lucia goes up to Jorge and looks at him meaningly.)* Do you know what I think? What's annoying you is that she pays so little attention to you.

He looks at her furiously, which seems to indicate that she has touched a sore spot... She moves away to the other side of the room, and at that moment Ramona comes in carrying a tureen of soup. Lucia leaves the room.

Jorge goes over to the table, sits down, and opens his napkin with irritation. Ramona has put the soup tureen on the edge of a sideboard. Jorge turns his back to her so that she has only to turn her head to see him. She gives him a look that is both tender and submissive. She is obviously disturbed by the presence of Don Jaime's son. Without taking her eyes off him, she goes to pick up the tureen again and prepares to bring it over to the table, but at that moment Lucia's voice is heard.

LUCIA: Ramona!

She starts as if she has been caught doing something wrong. For a moment she tries to catch the tureen, which is about to fall, but only succeeds in making matters worse. The soup tureen smashes onto the floor, its contents spreading out.

LUCIA: That's the last straw! What were you looking at, woman? Look what you've done!

Jorge has got up to look at the disaster. He looks at the maid, nodding his head in commiseration.

JORGE: So, Ramona!

LUCIA: Run and get something to mop it up with, quickly. *(Ramona obeys, fleeing. Lucia begins to pick up the pieces.)* That woman's getting more and more stupid every day.

Jorge sits down again, looking resigned.

JORGE: What of it!

The beggars' refectory, nighttime. The beggars are eating at a rough table made of planks. Surprisingly, they are respectably dressed. Their clothes are worn out but clean. Their appearance is relatively washed and tidy. Don Amalio, Poca, Don Zequiel, Hobbly, Enedina, and Refugio are there; also three other wretches, a man and two women. One of the women is a dwarf, the other, whom we will call the gardener, is a nondescript, middle-aged woman. The last character, who is named Paco, is a man of about fifty with a shaggy beard but no scar or physical deformity. They are all eating heartily.

DON AMALIO: When I wasn't so miserable I used to sell pigs. Begging your pardon, I was more honest than my holy Mother.

POCA *(swallowing)*: So you didn't come from the poorhouse!

The blind man puts his plate on the table and grasps his stick.

DON AMALIO: I'll hit whoever said that.

Don Amalio seems to mean what he says.

ENEDINA: Don't pay any attention to him, Don Amalio, he's a rogue.

Other voices are raised.

VOICES *(ad lib.)*: Good evening, miss *(etc., etc.)*.

Viridiana has just appeared on the threshold with two new guests, the woman singer and the leper.

DON ZEQUIEL *(standing up with respect)* : Benedictus!

Viridiana smiles at this incongruity. The singer looks distrustfully at the others; she didn't expect such a great number. The leper holds back as if uncertain of the reception he will receive. All keep silent for the moment and the noise of eating is heard. Viridiana makes the new guests sit down and gives them each a spoon and a plate.

VIRIDIANA: Make room for your new companions. You sit there, you there. I guess they're hungry, aren't they?

SINGER: God will reward you.

VIRIDIANA: Have you eaten well? Did you like it?

DON ZEQUIEL: I don't want to criticize the saintly miss who is so good to us, but I would take the liberty of saying that the beans were acid.

REFUGIO: What does that mean?

POCA: Sour, idiot.

REFUGIO: Don't pay any attention to them, they're peasants.

Viridiana silences them.

VIRIDIANA: If Don Zequiel says the beans were bad it must be true. We'll do something about it tomorrow.

They all look at the leper with disgust. Viridiana helps him to something and the man begins to eat hungrily. Viridiana places the bread basket near him.

VIRIDIANA *(smiling)* : Now I've got some good news for you. From tomorrow on everyone will have some work to do.

This is a disagreeable surprise. They look at each other. Poca is flabbergasted and terrified.

VIRIDIANA: Don't worry, you won't be asked to do anything impossible or anything you won't want to do. I only want you to have a bit of a change and to take some exercise.

ENEDINA: I'm a cook, miss, I'm good at roasts and vanilla puddings. Last year I made pastry for the Companza people. They can still remember it.

VIRIDIANA: Good. *(She goes up to each of them in turn. To the dwarf.)* You can help me with the accounts.

DWARF: Yes, miss.

HOBBLY: I can paint religious pictures... Before, I used to be able to write, but now with this leg I've forgotten...

PACO: I can weave hemp, but with the rheumatism in my fingers...

VIRIDIANA: What about you, Manuel?

POCA: I'm only good at making people laugh.

VIRIDIANA: That's all right; we all laugh here, but not at you; I'll see to that.

The leper is eating beside the woman gardener, who sees him stretch out his arm for a piece of bread.

GARDENER: I've got green fingers. The priest will tell you...

VIRIDIANA: So you won't get bored here, there'll be more than enough for you to do!

The gardener suddenly points to the leper's arm.

GARDENER: Look! It's disgusting.

He immediately conceals his arm. Everybody looks at him.

HOBBLY: Let's see it.

Poca, standing up to see better, tries to get a look at the sores.

GARDENER: That's leprosy.

REFUGIO: Throw him out, miss! We're all clean here.

Viridiana goes up to the leper, who has stood up, and calmly takes his arm. He resists a bit, but she succeeds in examining a sore. At her gesture they all fall silent and watch with revulsion.

LEPER: They're varicose veins, miss, but some days I can't take care of them.

VIRIDIANA: Are you sure it isn't contagious?

LEPER: They told me it isn't at the hospital.

VOICE: Don't listen to him, miss. I've known him for a long time.

The leper looks at his companions.

LEPER *(angrily)*: They're varicose veins. It isn't leprosy.

VIRIDIANA *(to all)*: I'll take him to the doctor tomorrow. Come on now, sit down and go on eating. And you, look after him as if he were a sick brother. Be understanding. Now finish eating and then go to bed. Everyone in bed by eight o'clock!

Viridiana shows the newcomers where to sleep. With varied inflections the beggars bid her good night. Hobbly goes to the door, opens it for Viridiana and wishes her good night. The leper sits down again in his place. Viridiana goes out.

Hobbly turns back and approaches the leper. He pushes him with his stick and motions him to get up.

HOBBLY: If you don't disappear I'll make holes in your belly.

LEPER *(frightened)*: You're not the one to make me move. *(Hobbly pulls out a knife.)* The miss, she understands, she told me I could stay.

There is a scuffle.

ENEDINA: Hit him if he doesn't get out!

The blind man beats the table with his stick.

DON AMALIO: Calm down, people, calm down. Somebody will get hurt. If anything happens, we'll all be thrown out.

SINGER: Out, the turd!

The leper relents and begins to leave.

LEPER: Okay, that's it, I give in, but I'm staying on the grounds. All together you'd be able... *(He begins to walk away, goes a few paces, but then turns around. He indicates the table, ashamed.)* Give me something for tomorrow morning.

The gardener, more compassionate than the others, takes a piece of bread and hands it to him at arm's length. The leper puts it in his pocket and goes to the . door.

The blind man, who has not left his place, has Enedina at his side. He is pawing her thighs. They whisper.

DON AMALIO: I'll come to you tonight.

ENEDINA: No, the children sleep with me.

DON AMALIO: Give them to Refugio.

ENEDINA: No, I don't want to because they yell. And I've got news for you too.

DON AMALIO: Then I'll get you in the fields tomorrow...

VOICE *(off)*: Pass me the salt.

They all get up. Hobbly sees Rita's jumprope on the table and takes it to tie up his trousers.

Viridiana's room. The room is lit by a candle. The young girl is kneeling on the floor like a countrywoman, telling her beads. There is a knock at the door.

VIRIDIANA: Who's there?

Without answering, Jorge comes into the room with a cigar between his lips. Looking annoyed, Viridiana gets up quickly.

VIRIDIANA: Jorge. You frightened me. What's happening to you?

JORGE: It's about time we spoke to each other, isn't it?

VIRIDIANA: Well... is it so urgent?

JORGE: If I wait until tomorrow it'll be the same as yesterday and the day before and all the other days. When you're not with your poor people, you're praying or you disappear, I never see you.

Both furious and ill at ease at being surprised, Viridiana rushes to the chest of drawers on top of which lie her wooden cross, the crown of thorns, and the hammer. She quickly hides them in a drawer.

VIRIDIANA: What's the matter?

JORGE *(off)*: I want to put in some electricity, change the habits... well, to make some improvements. *(Viridiana listens as if this were foreign to her.)* Then there's the land. It really hurts me to think of its not producing anything.

VIRIDIANA: I don't know anything about these things, Jorge...

JORGE: But you have a right to let us know what you think.

VIRIDIANA: I'm not interested. Do what you think's best. *(She steps forward as if to show that the conversation has come to an end.)* Is that everything?

Jorge has no intention of ending the conversation so abruptly. He goes on irritably.

JORGE: No, it isn't; there's much more. It seems absurd for us to be staying here so near each other in this situation without knowing each other. *(He plants himself near her and leans on the bed.)* What do you know about me?

VIRIDIANA: I know that you used to work with an architect.

JORGE: And do you know that my mother and I had to suffer? If my father had bothered himself a little more about us I'd be an architect now.

She does not reply and so does not encourage him to talk further. Jorge looks around with curiosity. He sits on the bed and is suddenly aware of its hardness. He punches the blanket. There is a board underneath instead of a mattress. Jorge underlines his discovery with irony.

JORGE: I don't understand how you can like being alone so much.

VIRIDIANA: I'm not like you, you have your wife.

This gives Jorge an opportunity to hurt her. He gets up and goes up behind her.

JORGE: We're not married. I don't need anybody's blessing to live with a woman. *(Viridiana does not blink. If she is embarrassed she does not show it.)* I see that you... I ought to go. Good night.

He goes to the door.

VIRIDIANA *(dryly)*: The next time you come, knock first and wait until I tell you to come in.

This remark, made perfectly naturally, produces an unexpected reaction in Jorge and restores all his aplomb. Before leaving he runs his eyes over the young woman's body. With a mocking smile he blows a puff of smoke toward her and leaves.

Viridiana locks the door with the key and brushes the smoke away with her hand. She goes to the window and opens it wide, to let in some air. Then she moves to the center of the room again, while the camera frames the open window.

The park. The singer is heard, off, humming a couplet. Close-up of a sheet of tin plate on which is painted in a very primitive style the scene of a miracle: a sick woman lying on a bed, with the Virgin and two angels on one side. The painter is adding the last touches to the face of the sick woman. We see the artist's arm, then his face: it is Hobbly. A few feet away, sitting on an old wheelbarrow, is the singer, who is posing for him. Behind her Enedina is hanging out laundry on a line.

HOBBLY: I'll put some yellow in her face to show she is ill.

SINGER: Hurry up, I'm cramped all over.

HOBBLY: It's nearly finished, sweetheart.

In the background, from near the house, Don Amalio approaches, led by Refugio.

SINGER: I don't like having to stay still for so long.

HOBBLY: It seems to me that you ought to know damn well how to swing your...

Viridiana appears a few yards behind the painter with Poca; both come forward to inspect the painting. Poca looks at the masterpiece and begins to laugh.

POCA *(referring to the sick woman)*: She looks like a sick marrow!

VIRIDIANA: Don't pay any attention to him. It's very good.

SINGER: I don't like having to be the Virgin.

HOBBLY: You ought to be the one in bed. I'd like to ask you, miss, to pose…

Hobbly stands up in his turn.

VIRIDIANA *(amused)* : Me?

HOBBLY: Come on, miss. Just so the Virgin can be really pretty.

(Viridiana doesn't seem convinced. Hobbly insists.) It won't take but a minute. It's a votive offering for a lady who was cured just when she was dying of fever. Our Lady of the Helpless granted her a favor.

VIRIDIANA: Do you have great devotion for the Virgin?

Hobbly sits down again.

HOBBLY: I'm not a bigot, miss, but everybody has his own beliefs... and then... with this terrible thing *(points to his legs)*, if I didn't have faith...

Viridiana is sitting on a wheelbarrow. Near by Refugio is adjusting Don Amalio's clothes.

VIRIDIANA *(to Refugio)* : I must know when you expect to give birth.

REFUGIO: Why?

VIRIDIANA: Heavens! So the doctor can be warned.

REFUGIO: In that case in about four months, but I can't tell you exactly.

POCA *(chiming in insolently)* : She doesn't even know who the father was. She said that it was night and she couldn't even see his head.

REFUGIO *(vexed)* : I didn't expect you to scream it from the house tops.

DON AMALIO *(with authority)* : Shut up. You shouldn't speak like that in front of our holy protector who is a well-bred person.

Viridiana gets up and arranges Refugio's clothes. She is astonished. She had never imagined that such people existed. She finds this contact with decadence both seductive and horrifying.

VIRIDIANA *(to Refugio)* : I'm very sorry for you. Have you any other children?

REFUGIO: No, miss, it will be the first. Do you mind...?

Viridiana sits down again. At that moment Don Zequiel, the bearded patriarch, and the dwarf arrive. Hobbly continues working. Viridiana is posing. The others are silent.

DWARF: We're going to the village, miss...

DON ZEQUIEL: With God's and your own permission.

ENEDINA *(to Viridiana)* : They must bring me some potatoes, bacon, and rice.

Viridiana gives Don Zequiel some money.

VIRIDIANA: Take it and be careful not to be as late as you were yesterday.

DON AMALIO *(with a sickly smile)* : Could they bring me some tobacco?

POCA : No, miss. Smoking makes him spit and feel ill.

DON AMALIO *(furiously)* : Smoking makes me feel ill? It's these filthy fag ends. I won't mention in this company what's upsetting you... or...

VIRIDIANA *(conciliatory)* : That'll do. Bring the tobacco and I'll distribute it.

DON AMALIO : Thank you, miss.

The dwarf and Don Zequiel leave.

HOBBLY *(off)* : Come over here and see the picture.

He has finished his work. Viridiana gets up and goes over to see the result. All of them gather around to look at the artist's work.

VIRIDIANA : It's very good.

HOBBLY : Thank you; but it's missing something.

VIRIDIANA : That doesn't matter; I like it.

A road bordering on Don Jaime's property. Jorge and his foreman are standing near an electric pole. They are measuring the ground with a tape.

JORGE : How much is that?

FOREMAN : Fifteen yards.

JORGE : That's fifteen by seven?

FOREMAN : That's it.

JORGE : Good.

Jorge jots the figures down in his little notebook and rolls up the tape. They are both walking toward the road. A little covered wagon pulled by a mule is coming along the road in their direction. The wagon passes. Inside it, under the canvas, are two policemen in uniform and another man. Behind them the driver's back is visible. A dog is attached to the axle of the wagon by about three feet of string.

The dog runs along panting, its tongue hanging out. It seems to be exhausted and can hardly keep up with the mule. If it stopped, it would be pulled along and strangled by the rope.

The dog recedes from the camera, framed between the two threatening wheels of the wagon. It reaches Jorge and passes him and his companion. The wagon stops at a fork in the road about a hundred yards farther on. Jorge goes toward it, intrigued. As he approaches, the two policemen jump down and speak to the owner of the wagon, who has got down on the other side.

ONE POLICEMAN: Thanks, pal, see you later.

PEASANT: Goodbye: if you ever need anything...

The two policemen go off. The peasant goes in back of the wagon to inspect the brakes. Jorge, sickened by the cruelty of the scene, comes up to the wagon. He is frowning and speaks harshly to the peasant.

JORGE: That animal can't take any more. Now that the wagon's empty, why don't you let him ride?

The peasant straightens up and stares at Jorge.

PEASANT: It's for people!

JORGE: Then let him go and he'll follow you.

PEASANT: And let him get run over by somebody else?

The apparent contrast between the peasant's cruelty and his care for the dog bewilders Jorge. He bends down and strokes the animal.

JORGE: I'll buy him.

The peasant looks at him for a moment. He is perplexed but reacts immediately.

PEASANT: He's good at rabbiting and he knows it. When we're in the country, if he doesn't hunt he doesn't get fed.

JORGE: How much do you want for him?

PEASANT *(hesitating)*: I wasn't thinking of selling him, but if you want... I'll leave it to you.

Jorge pulls some notes out of his pockets and gives two to the peasant.

JORGE: All right, untie him.

The peasant does so and hands the string, which is used as a lead, to Jorge.

PEASANT: Thank you, and God keep you and bless you. *(He taps the wagon and addresses the driver.)* Get moving. *(He gets onto the wagon and sits down where the policemen had been. The wagon moves off. To Jorge.)* And remember, the less he eats, the better he runs.

JORGE *(as the cart is going away)*: What's he called?

PEASANT *(shouting)*: Canelo!

On hearing his name the dog tries to jump toward his master, but Jorge pulls him back with the string.

JORGE: Be quiet! Where are you going? Come here, Canelo! Canelo! Come on!

Jorge and his companion leave the road and cross the field toward their workers. The wagon continues on its way. Another carriage comes from the opposite direction toward the camera. Neither Jorge nor the foreman pays any attention to it.

The second carriage, with another miserable dog attached to its axle, passes in front of the camera. The two men do not notice the unhappy dog as the cart goes by.

In the field two or three workmen are loading a truck with stones. Beyond them about twenty farm workers are clearing the land for plowing. It is full of stones and brushwood. They are wielding hoes and mattocks and tearing out bushes and weeds. Jorge and the foreman stop to watch the men work.

FOREMAN: Have you thought of what you want planted yet?

JORGE: The fields have been left so long; with a good manuring anything will grow.

FOREMAN: It's for wheat. We've always grown maize in the strip above the vegetables.

JORGE: And in the vegetable plot?

FOREMAN: That's good land.

Suddenly the young man sees Viridiana passing near by on the road. Viridiana comes up, followed by Poca. She is holding a white box which she had near her when she was posing for Hobbly's picture a short time before. Jorge goes forward to meet her.

JORGE: What a miracle, you let yourself be seen. Have you come to look at the work?

Poca passes discreetly, giving Jorge a wide berth to avoid meeting him.

VIRIDIANA: I've told you before I'm not interested in this.

Jorge looks around with the satisfied expression of a landlord.

JORGE: The best thing my father left me was the land. You can see the result of the work on it, and if you helped me it wouldn't take long to change it even more. *(Viridiana does not reply and tries to move on. To Poca.)* What are you doing here? Get out.

VIRIDIANA *(off)*: Leave him alone.

JORGE: You won't get much done with those people. Those times are over! You ought to let me kick them out.

VIRIDIANA: Do they worry you that much, then?

JORGE: They worry me a great deal, and especially because of you.

Viridiana keeps walking. Jorge walks beside her. He still has the dog with him.

JORGE: There's no point in helping some of them when there are so many others.

VIRIDIANA: I know perfectly well how little I can do. What I want

to do is give passing beggars a roof, some food, and a bit of human warmth.

JORGE: Is that all you're going to devote your life to?

VIRIDIANA: I'm not sure yet. I've had a shock recently, and I'm only beginning to get over it. Perhaps I'll go back to the convent one day.

At this point there is a strange intermittent noise as if a bit of tin plate were being knocked against stones. There is also shouting.

WORKMEN'S VOICES *(shouting)* : Put your things somewhere else! Get out of here!

Viridiana looks toward the commotion. The leper comes up. He is afraid to come too close to her because of the people who are there. He is pulling along an empty can which is attached to his belt by a piece of string : it is the can hitting against the stones which is making the noise. On hearing the shouts of the workmen, the beggar reacts with gestures of contempt.

LEPER: Swine.

VIRIDIANA *(off)* : Why are they shouting at him? Haven't they any pity?

Jorge, who has witnessed this scene, shrugs his shoulders.

JORGE: I don't know what's going on; ask him.

Viridiana goes to the leper. The cruel mocking of the workmen can still be heard. The foreman goes up to Jorge, smiling.

FOREMAN: These rascals are demons. They've tied a can to him. Because they find the poor guy revolting they make him walk with this can so they know when he's coming.

Viridiana, with Poca just behind her, goes up to the leper and unties the can while she is talking.

VIRIDIANA: Why did you come here, José? I told you where to go until you're cured.

José the leper kicks the can away angrily.

LEPER: The weather is wonderful, the sun is warm, so I keep on walking and walking... then you see...

Viridiana doesn't reproach him, on the contrary she replies gently.

VIRIDIANA: How are you today?

LEPER: Things seem to be getting better.

VIRIDIANA: Hold your arm out. You can't hope to be cured quickly.

You heard what the doctor said. If it had been seen to in time... This'll take time. But with the help of God, we'll pull through.

They go up to a clump of trees. Poca keeps his distance and then hides behind a bush. Jorge, very unhappy, watches them go. But he recovers immediately and goes up to the workmen. Viridiana sits down on a big stone and makes the leper sit beside her.

VIRIDIANA: Stretch out your arm.

While he is obeying, she takes a tube of ointment and some gauze from the box she is carrying. She begins to treat the arm. During this process the leper talks.

LEPER: It all started one unlucky day. A punishment from God

because one windy day I was with a woman and after that I started to be punished. You're the first good woman I've seen; if all women were as bad as the priests say, you wouldn't take care of me. You, bad?

He shakes his head and laughs stupidly. Viridiana does not seem to hear and goes on with her task calmly.

VIRIDIANA: Are your parents alive?

LEPER: Parents? Nobody cares a damn, what's the use of them?

VIRIDIANA: Don't say that.

LEPER: Right, I won't say that, but I still think they're no use.

Poca, who has been listening to the conversation, comes out of hiding and intervenes angrily. He waves his arms around like a windmill.

POCA: Don't pay any attention, miss; this man's no good. He wants you to catch it too. At church he puts his arm into the Holy Water and seems to say would to God all those damn women got it. The priest won't let him in.

The leper gets up mad with rage. The young woman can hardly hold him back.

LEPER: You'll soon find out, you liar!

VIRIDIANA: Stop this!

LEPER: He's lying through his arse!

POCA: Ask the priest, miss.

VIRIDIANA: That's enough. (*To Poca.*) Go join the others, and don't come back here. (*To the leper.*) And you'll have to control your temper.

Peace reigns. Poca leaves, annoyed. Viridiana finishes bandaging the leper's arm. He bows his head, not daring to protest, in spite of his urge to do so.

Don Jaime's room at night. An oil lamp is burning. Jorge is sitting at a table holding an old gold watch. He is winding it carefully. His face expresses curiosity and pleasure.

JORGE *(looking at the watch):* This must have been my grand-
father's.

Lucia is getting ready for bed. She is sitting on the edge of the bed in her nightgown. There is an atmosphere of cold conjugal routine.

JORGE: If you wake first, wake me up.

LUCIA: What are you going to do?

She gets up and comes over to him.

JORGE: What I do every day, but I want to do it earlier.

LUCIA *(slightly reproachful):* You're happy, aren't you?

Jorge inserts a little gold key into the watch.

JORGE: Shouldn't I be? You, on the other hand…

LUCIA: I'm bored. I'm alone all day and I don't know what to do.

JORGE: You should have enough to do in this house… Come here and listen to this.

She comes to him and he puts the watch to her ear, winding a little spring. A tiny chime is heard. He is pleased with his discovery. She listens, frowning. The tiny musical sound stops.

JORGE: What are you thinking about?

LUCIA *(harshly)*: That your cousin is more to your taste.

Jorge is startled. He hesitates, then tries to change the subject.

JORGE: She isn't my cousin.

LUCIA: It doesn't make any difference what she is: you like her. *(Jorge puts the watch in a box.)* I had a feeling I shouldn't have come here. I'd better get out, fast…

She goes back to the bed. Jorge, who does not like the way this conversation is going, wants to divert it.

JORGE: We ought to talk about that some other time. *(She gets into bed. Jorge, paying no attention, continues to play with the watch.)* How in hell does it wind up?

LUCIA: I think I'd better go tomorrow.

JORGE: Don't be a fool! Why rush away from something which couldn't happen?

He hums. Lucia slips between the sheets.

LUCIA: You see how much you like her!

JORGE: That's life. Some people are brought together, others are separated. What can we do, if that's the way it happens?

(Lucia, under the blankets, sobs.) Lucia! Don't cry! Come on, darling, don't cry like that!

He is still very busy with his father's trinkets. He suddenly comes across a small jeweled crucifix. With his left hand, he gets hold of the little blade which is set into one side of it: the crucifix is in fact the handle of a dagger.

JORGE: What a thing! Where did Father find that?

Lucia is still sobbing. Jorge tries to open a watch case with the point of the dagger.

A hundred yards behind the house there is a small wood in which there are several buildings, mostly in ruins, all scattered. One of them serves as the living quarters and dormitory of the beggars. Another building, in equally bad repair, is some sort of storehouse where a group of about fifteen masons and laborers are working. A truck is standing in the yard with a load of materials; the foreman is supervising the unloading. Jorge comes out of the house with Canelo, still on the end of the string.

JORGE *(pointing to the truck)*: Hold on, Ramon! Is there time to make another trip?

FOREMAN: No, sir, it's nearly six o'clock. *(To the workmen who are unloading the truck.)* Okay, let's get a move on! *(To Jorge.)* When are you leaving?

JORGE: Tonight, but I'll be back tomorrow afternoon.

The village clock chimes six.

About three hundred feet from the work yard there are rows of almond trees. Most of Viridiana's beggars are sitting there on the ground or standing around. The blind man comes from the path, led by the dwarf. From afar the six strokes of the village clock finish chiming. Viridiana arrives. She claps her hands.

VIRIDIANA: The Angelus.

Hurrying the beggars kneel, with the exception of Hobbly who remains

standing, leaning on his stick. Viridiana also remains standing. The leper, seeing what is happening, moves quickly past the group and goes away. In a quick montage, there follow alternated shots of the beggars praying quietly under the blossoms of the almond trees and the work in full swing: close-up of cement slapped onto a dilapidated wall, a tub full of water in which some lime falls, sand being sifted, logs piling up on the ground, a wheelbarrow full of stones being tipped out, planks beings sawed. The sounds underline the contrast: the otherworldly muttering of Viridiana and the beggars; the very actual and rhythmic sound of the activity in the work yard.

VIRIDIANA *(praying)* : The Angel of the Lord declared to Mary.

There is a subdued murmur in which the voices of women, who are more familiar with the words, are prominent.

BEGGARS: And she conceived by the Holy Ghost.

ALL: Hail Mary full of grace the Lord is with thee blessed art thou amongst women and blessed is the fruit of thy womb Jesus. Holy Mary Mother of God pray for us sinners now and at the hour of our death. Amen.

The camera moves to dump truck noisily emptying its load onto the ground. Two masons are stacking bricks. The beggars are heard in the distance reciting the Hail Mary. Jorge walks in front of a heap of cement and sand, where there are two men shoveling.

VIRIDIANA'S VOICE: Behold the handmaid of the Lord.

BEGGARS' VOICES: Be it done unto me according to thy word. Hail Mary full of grace...

VIRIDIANA'S VOICE: And the word was made flesh.

BEGGARS' VOICES: And dwelt among us. Hail Mary full of grace...

The camera shifts back to Viridiana in prayer. She prays without ostentation, very simply. A few feet away from her, Hobbly leans on his stick contemplatively.

VIRIDIANA: Pray for us, O Holy Mother of God.

BEGGARS: That we may be made worthy of the promises of Christ.

The beggars cross themselves, stand up, and go away. Viridiana walks in the direction of the work yard.

Jorge sees the young woman coming toward him smiling. He feels sorry for her. To a man of action like himself, his feet well on the ground, Viridiana seems to be behaving absurdly : but he is strongly attacted by her gentleness and beauty.

As the two young people approach each other, the workers and the foreman, who have finished work and changed their clothes, come out of the building and pass in front of them. They wave to Jorge and leave.

VIRIDIANA *(indicating the building and the beggars' house)*: Are they going to work here too?

JORGE: Don't worry. Nobody's going to disturb you.

His eyes run quickly over her body. He can't hide the ironic reaction he experiences upon completing this examination.

JORGE: Don't forget the meeting with the lawyer. The car will pick you up tomorrow morning.

VIRIDIANA: I'll be ready.

JORGE *(nodding toward the dormitories)*: Do you intend to stay here for some time?

The beggars pass to and fro.

VIRIDIANA: Yes. Why?

JORGE: You can come and live again in the big house if you want. Now that I'm alone I can settle down anywhere.

Viridiana lowers her eyes shyly.

VIRIDIANA: And... your friend?

JORGE: She's left.

VIRIDIANA: Is she coming back?

JORGE: No.

VIRIDIANA: Why?

Jorge stares at her with a certain amount of insolence.

JORGE: Why does any man leave a woman? *(She shrugs and purses her lips, indicating her lack of experience.)* If you don't understand I don't want to explain it to you. You're too cold and religious; you'd be shocked.

Viridiana blushes. He bursts out laughing and walks off toward the work yard.

VOICE *(off)*: Miss!

Old Moncho and the coachman-cum-farmhand, looking awkward, are waiting near by. Viridiana goes up to them. We can see Ramona's back behind them. She is fidgeting with a bunch of keys. She seems to be waiting for something.

VIRIDIANA: You have decided to leave, Moncho.

MONCHO: Yes!

VIRIDIANA: I can't do anything to make you stay? These people annoy you, isn't that it? *(The two men don't answer but look down.)* Well, what are you going to do?

Jorge passes near the group and goes to Ramona.

COACHMAN: He's coming to live with me, miss.

VIRIDIANA: If that's what you want... But I'm very sorry you're leaving. Thank you for everything, Moncho. God bless you.

She shakes hands with them. They go off toward the village. Ramona hands Jorge the bunch of keys when he comes up to her. Without saying anything they go off toward the house.

The attic at the top of the house. There is a bizarre collection of junk: an ancient worm-eaten piano, some old suitcases, some broken chairs, various boxes, unsteady-looking piles of crates, a burst mattress, a once elegant couch, now torn and dirty. The voices of Jorge and Ramona are heard coming from another room.

JORGE'S VOICE: Obviously! Here's the missing furniture! What a state it's in! Father must have been a peculiar type.

RAMONA'S VOICE: I don't think the master ever came here.

They both appear. Jorge is carrying the keys Ramona gave him earlier, in the field. He looks at the couch cover.

JORGE: And this chest?

RAMONA: There are some curtains and drapes, but they're all very old.

A cat makes its way through the piled-up crates.

JORGE: There must be some rat's nest in there! I'd like to ask you something. You worked for my father for seven years, didn't you? Did he ever mention me?

Ramona's eyes follow him tenderly.

RAMONA: I don't know; I can't remember. But I'm sure he loved you.

JORGE: Why?

RAMONA: You wouldn't be here otherwise.

JORGE *(hitting a chair):* These chairs are in good condition. With a little varnish and some new covers this one will be quite presentable.

Jorge continues to poke around. Again Ramona looks at him with the willing submission evident before. Jorge goes to another corner of the attic, where on one side sacks are heaped against the wall. The camera frames a door and a few beams. Jorge goes up to a heap of sacks.

JORGE: What are these sacks doing here?

He half lifts them.

RAMONA: I don't know—they've always been there.

JORGE: That's stupid! Plaster! It can still be used. *(He goes up to another pile of sacks. Ramona follows him, fascinated.)* And those? That's sand. As I won't be here tomorrow, tell the foreman to take them.

He shows the sacks to Ramona. Turning suddenly, his eyes meet hers. He understands everything. Frightened by the discovery, she avoids his glance. Jorge begins to laugh.

JORGE: What's wrong with you, woman? Why are you looking at me like that?

Ramona tries to escape, but the young man catches her by the arm. He pulls her around to face him and looks at her for a moment, in silence, smiling. Then he holds her chin.

JORGE: Do you know something, Ramona? If you took some trouble, you'd be quite pretty... Small teeth, a good mouth —what more do you want?

Without further ado, he kisses her on the lips, not even bothering to hold her. Feeling his lips on hers, she shuts her eyes. Her eyelids quiver. She gives herself up to the long awaited pleasure. Jorge looks around.

JORGE *(pulling her with him)* : Let's sit down a moment.

They go over to a pile of sacks.

Close-up of the piled-up furniture. The camera frames a big rat busy by an old sack. With a bound the cat is on it.

A car stops in front of the house, near Viridiana, who is waiting. The driver gets out.

VIRIDIANA: Are we leaving?

DRIVER: Don Jorge said he'd be waiting for you at the lawyer's at four o'clock.

VIRIDIANA: Good. *(She goes up to Don Zequiel and the singer, who are waiting near by. To Don Zequiel.)* You're the most responsible here. I'm handing them over to you. Make sure they all behave themselves.

DON ZEQUIEL *(off)* : Don't worry, miss, I'll look after things.

VIRIDIANA *(off)* : Do you want anything else?

DON ZEQUIEL *(off)* : Bring me a flute if you see one. I'd like to learn music.

Ramona, together with Rita who has her face bandaged as if she has a toothache, comes out of the house and shuts the door.

RITA *(weeping)* : They're going to hurt me.

RAMONA: Well if they hurt you, put up with it! Let's go!

Ramona and Rita get into the car, followed by Viridiana.

BEGGARS' VOICES: Good luck, miss!

The kitchen. Enedina is cradling her yelling baby in her arms.

DON AMALIO: Keep quiet. These miserable brats only get in the way.

ENEDINA: You'd like me to kill them?

POCA: With the life that's ahead of them they'd be better off being sent to Paradise.

Enedina goes up to Paco and hands him the child.

ENEDINA: Put her in the sun with her sister.

Paco takes the little girl, who is still crying, and leaves. Hobbly, who has been standing at the door watching the car go, comes back into the kitchen rubbing his hands.

HOBBLY: Now to knock off a couple of lambs. We'll have them roasted. *This idea obviously amazes Enedina. She looks at the blind man and Poca, who are enjoying themselves.* What do you think of that?

DON AMALIO: I'll go along with it... if it's being respectful enough.

ENEDINA: What will the lady say?

POCA: She won't even know.

ENEDINA: If everybody agrees, but to make a roast takes four hours.

HOBBLY: Well, what's all the hurry?

The blind man turns to Enedina.

DON AMALIO: Didn't you say you know how to make vanilla pudding?

ENEDINA: Yes, yes.

HOBBLY: You hear that, Poca? Get the eggs and milk. I'll see to the lambs.

Poca takes a pail and Paco hands him a basket. The blind man sits down on a bench and breaks out into merry idiotic laughter.

The park. Refugio, the pregnant woman, is busy collecting dead wood. The singer is sitting near her on a bench. She sings a few bars of a song in a grating voice, accompanying herself on a guitar. Don Zequiel is not far away. Unlike her normal self, Refugio is very active. She moves with great ease. The singer interrupts her song and addresses her companion.

SINGER: Don't kill yourself, Refugio! Can't you see we're alone?

REFUGIO: What's that got to do with it?

SINGER: What's the good of working?

Don Zequiel, scandalized, goes up to them.

DON ZEQUIEL: You keep quiet. The miss left me in charge here and nobody is going to upset things. You, stick to your singing!

SINGER: Look at us now! What made you think that I was up to something?

There are shouts from the house. They look around. The dwarf and the gardener are gesturing from the doorway.

GARDENER: Don Zequiel! Refugio! Come here!

DON ZEQUIEL: Damn women! How did you get in there?

DWARF: Through a back window.

Refugio and the gardener rush toward the house. Don Zequiel follows them uncertrainly.

DON ZEQUIEL: Where are you going?

The singer has reached the door.

SINGER: Come here, Don Zequiel. I was here with the lady. There're wonderful things inside!

Don Zequiel seems unconvinced.

DON ZEQUIEL: If it's only to have a look... *(He moves toward the house.)* But don't touch anything. Leave everything where it is!

The three beggars, one behind another, itching to have what has been forbidden them, join the others in the house.

The field. Close-up of a dove working it's way awkwardly over the grass. The leper, who is following it, throws himself forward and traps it in his hands.

LEPER: Little dove from the south, you're hurt. What are you called? *(He strokes it.)* My little dove! My dear dove! My darling, sweet dove!

Suddenly he is struck on the shoulder by a stone. He gets to his feet. Without realizing it, he has come to the place where the men are working. The laborers have seen him and are warning him in this crude way.

FIRST WORKER: Get out!

SECOND WORKER: Come any nearer and I'll bust your head in!

THIRD WORKER: Get lost.

One of them picks up a stone and hurls it at him. The leper, furious, makes obscene gestures at them and pours out insults while he rubs the place where the stone hit him.

LEPER: You bastards! I hope you get what I've got!

But while he is shouting, he is making off. Foaming with rage, he disappears into the trees, jabbering incoherently.

Interior of the sitting room. Close-up of the portrait of Doña Elvira. While the camera pulls back to include the portrait of Don Jaime, the comments of the beggars, who have just come into the house, are heard off.

SINGER: That woman, the one who looks like our Miss Viridiana, she's the wife of the man who hanged himself.

Among the first group of beggars, Don Zequiel is in the act of filling one of Don Jaime's pipes.

DON ZEQUIEL: Think of hanging yourself, with all that money!

SINGER: He must have had asthma. All those loaded old men have asthma.

They stop examining the picture and begin exploring the drawing room. The women go up to the cupboard which holds tablecloths and silver. The singer opens it. They stand, gaping.

DWARF: What stuff!

GARDENER: Jesus, Mary, and Joseph.

The singer takes out a heavily embroidered tablecloth which she has seen among others at the bottom of the cupboard. Don Zequiel, smoking the pipe, comes up to look.

SINGER: Look at that. How's that for a tablecloth?

GARDENER: Come on, let's put it out.

Excited, she puts it on the table and begins to spread it. The others help her.

REFUGIO: That must have cost a fortune. At least a thousand.

SINGER: A thousand! More like ten thousand! Can't you see it's French lace!

DON ZEQUIEL: Go on, fold it up, you're going to spoil it.

SINGER: Keep on smoking and shut up. We're not doing any harm. It's not as bad as smoking his tobacco.

REFUGIO: Don Zequiel's right. If those people come back and we don't hear them, God help you.

GARDENER: They won't get back before tomorrow. I heard them tell the driver.

REFUGIO: If you haven't eaten on lace like that you haven't lived.

The dining room that night. Close-up of a shaking hand trying to pick up a full glass of wine from the laid table. The sumptuous tablecloth is stained with wine and grease. The hand knocks the glass over. Scraps of talk are heard.

VOICE *(off)*: Watch it, Don Zequiel!

REFUGIO: Don't worry! We'll all clean it up; it'll be as right as rain.

The camera reveals an extraordinary scene. The beggars are sitting at the table; the leper is by himself at a small adjacent table. They have got through two roast lambs, the remains of which are scattered over the table. There is an extraordinary confusion of glasses, plates, and bottles; the "guests" are unhampered by any formality, and some of them—like the patriarchal Don Zequiel, who has just knocked over the glass—are really drunk, others only "lit-up."

PACO: Pass me that bottle.

SINGER: Go on, Don Amalio!

DON AMALIO: They've got a real hen house here! You can't hear yourself speak.

POCA: Tell me the answer to this! What bird lays eggs in a barn?

VOICE: Shut up, let's hear Don Amalio!

DON AMALIO: Quiet! Now we're gathered together to beg under the porches. But only in the churches of the rich! The girls passing by smelled so sweet that you felt them on you.

Poca is chewing a hunk of mutton. His hands and chin are shiny with fat.

POCA: That's great! You can smell them but you can't lay your hands on them! Is that it?

The leper is sitting some feet away from the others, but as the drinking goes on he gradually works his way in until finally he joins the group; the others are beyond noticing his sores. The leper claps his hands to show his appreciation of the blind man's story.

LEPER: Why did you split up?

Don Amalio grimaces at the sound of the leper's voice. He half turns toward him.

DON AMALIO: You, shut your face! I won't have questions from anyone!

Most of them are not listening; they are talking to each other, eating noisily, pouring out wine for themselves and each other.

VOICE *(off)*: Go on with the story!

DON AMALIO *(heavily)*: Okay, it broke up when this deaf fellow started on the collection boxes in the churches with a knife.

Enedina has finished eating and is picking her teeth with her fingers, unconcernedly.

SINGER: How did you know?

DON AMALIO: The noise of the money in his pocket gave him away. We hardly got a sou that day. *(He strikes the table to get silence and attention.)* You know what I did? I told the police about him!

HOBBLY: You sang because he didn't cut you in, you rat!

The blind man reacts, seizing his stick. Then he decides to talk his way out.

DON AMALIO: The judges thanked me very much, and one of them, who was a gentleman, said I was...

The old man, Don Zequiel, who is half slumped over the table, comes around sufficiently to pick up the blind man's story.

DON ZEQUIEL *(muttering)* : Shitty bastard, that's what I'd call you!

Don Amalio goes on as if he has not heard. The singer, his neighbor, leaves the table.

DON AMALIO : He said "Honest citizen," if you want to know.

The singer takes up her guitar and begins to sing a popular song. Most of them join in. Don Zequiel is slumped over the table, trying to sleep. Poca is drinking heavily with one of the women. One of Enedina's daughters, who is sleeping on a couch, wakes up frightened and begins to bawl. Refugio, who is tight, cannot bear the din and lurches toward the little girl.

REFUGIO *(shouting)* : You filthy little brat. Shut up or watch out! *(She picks up the whining child and shakes her brutally.)* What's up with you? Why are you screaming? I'll belt you one!

Enedina rushes up furiously and takes the child out of her arms.

ENEDINA : Don't you touch my little girl.

REFUGIO : Keep the brat quiet so we can hear what's going on.

ENEDINA : I'll bust your face.

REFUGIO : Keep your hands off me, you filthy tart!

Enedina hits her powerfully. Refugio jumps on her like a tigress and grabs her hair. The crying of the children gets louder. The others go on singing, apparently unperturbed by the fight. The two women hit each other in a blind fury. Poca and Paco try in vain to separate them, under the glassy stare of Don Zequiel. But it takes Don Amalio to calm them. He takes Enedina and protects her with his body.

DON AMALIO : Stop this, stop this.

ENEDINA : Let me go, Don Amalio, I'll tear her apart.

During the brawl the leper goes up to the table to get a bottle. Hobbly, without leaving his place, pokes him viciously with his stick.

Don Amalio does not let Enedina go.

DON AMALIO: Keep quiet, Enedina, she's not worth paying attention to. Let's behave ourselves nicely. *(To Refugio.)* Stick to your place.

There is calm once again. They all go back to their places and adjust their clothes.

Poca goes up to the sideboard where he finds the plate of vanilla pudding. He sticks in his finger and licks it greedily.

ENEDINA *(off)*: My pudding! Leave it, you thief!

She pushes Poca's hand into the plate. He pulls it out covered with cream.

VOICES *(off)*: Bring in the pudding, enough of the brawling.

Enedina, still puffing and blowing, takes the plate of pudding, walks to the table, and puts the pudding down. There are claps and murmurs of satisfaction. There is no more singing. The children are quiet. They all help themselves to pudding and there is quiet while they all taste the dessert. The leper prowls around the table with a plate in his hand, not daring to take any. Once again Hobbly drives him away. The gardener realizes what is going on, fills a plate and brings it to him. Then she sits down again and helps herself. Poca catches Enedina's eye.

POCA: Enedina?

ENEDINA *(off)*: What do you want?

POCA: Is it all right?

ENEDINA: Yes.

POCA *(addressing all of them)*: Enedina's going to take a picture. So we'll have a souvenir.

DON AMALIO: Where's the camera?

ENEDINA *(laughing cagily)*: It's a present from my parents.

They go to one side of the table. The leper places himself near the blind man, who sits in the middle. The blind man sits very straight, with his arms stretched out and his two hands on the table. The others arrange themselves on either side of him, striking different poses. In honor of the occasion Don Zequiel has come out of his stupor. When everyone is ready Enedina stands in front of them. She turns her back to the camera. In a flash the still scene suddenly conjures up the scene of another Supper.

Enedina sweeps her very ample skirt up to her face. The photograph is taken. She chokes with laughter behind her skirt. They all relax their poses and break out into disordered babbling. The group comes to life again and the hubbub reigns supreme.

The leper now appears lecherous and gay. He goes up to the phonograph. takes a record, puts it down dissatisfied, and then picks up another at random. He puts it on the record player. It is the Hallelujah Chorus from Handel's Messiah. He plays it very loud and this seems to give him pleasure *and even more strength. He glides toward Don Jaime's room. Before going in, he looks at them defiantly but they don't seem to notice.*

Enedina helps shake Don Zequiel, who has fallen asleep again.

REFUGIO: The lousy man. Tables aren't meant to lie on.

SINGER: Eat your pudding. It's a dream.

Handel's music fills the room with sound. Don Zequiel opens an eye and looks bleary. He sees the plate which is being handed to him. The singer, laughing, spoon-feeds him like a child.

DON ZEQUIEL *(half unconscious)* : You're a dainty piece. How spry you are, Enedina.

They all burst out laughing.

SINGER : This isn't Enedina.

In the middle of the hubbub the leper appears at the door of Don Jaime's room in Doña Elvira's veil and corset. He begins to dance to the music of the Hallelujah Chorus. It is a wild grotesque dance, with movements of the fandango and an expression of inane merriment. His incongruous toothless mouth makes it slightly sinister. He pulls tufts of feathers out from his jacket and throws them around the room onto the guests. His entry causes some surprise. The women scream and the men jeer. Soon the singer gets up and goes to dance with the leper. She takes of his veil and puts it around herself. It begins to look like a witches' sabbath.

LEPER *(throwing the feathers)* : Little dove of the south. Little dove.

The blind man, still sitting, pulls Enedina onto his knee.

DON AMALIO: Enedina, come here. Sit down. Come on, drink up!

Enedina drinks.

Poca joins the others. He pulls his beret over his eyes and goes into a series of contortions, moving his arms and legs with a frenzied agility remarkable for a man of his age, gyrating in a mad jig. He dances with the gardener. Refugio joins in to dance with the leper, keeping her distance, however.

While the couples are dancing, Hobbly, Don Zequiel, and Don Amalio still sit around the table. One of Enedina's little girls has begun to cry again. Don Zequiel, who has finished his dessert, contemplates the show without understanding clearly what is going on.

Enedina goes to the couch, carrying the weeping little girl in her arms.

ENEDINA: There, there, don't cry.

She puts the child on the couch; the crying stops. Paco appears behind the couch, gesturing to Enedina, and points to where he is.

PACO: Look at this, Enedina.

Enedina goes around the couch to Paco, curious to see what it is.

ENEDINA: What is it?

PACO: Get down, you won't see it otherwise.

The woman does so. Paco grabs her and makes her fall behind the couch; they roll over each other. Their legs stick out behind one end of the couch. Sometimes hers are on top, sometimes his. They roll around on the floor, Paco laughing, Enedina protesting. The gardener sees what is happening behind the couch and waves Don Zequiel over.

GARDENER: Just look at this, Don Zequiel! Isn't it awful!

He looks and sees. The legs of the couple struggle behind the couch. Close-up of the scared face of the little child stretched out on the couch.

ENEDINA'S VOICE: Get off, let me go! Let me go! Let me go!

Don Zequiel vigorously thumps the table.

DON ZEQUIEL: Leave them alone! It'll make them sorrier later!

Hobbly hurls a plate of pudding into the "patriarch's" face. Don Zequiel wipes his face with his hands, trying to get the stuff off his beard. Meanwhile, Poca, who has just seen what is happening behind the couch, passes near Don Zequiel and laughs at the state he is in.

GARDENER *(off):* That's just the thing for you, Don Zequiel! Ecce Homo, that's what I'd say!

Don Zequiel tries to get to his feet to defend himself, but he wobbles and falls back heavily onto his chair. Poca, who is looking cautiously over his shoulder, comes up to Don Amalio who is still in his place and touches him on the shoulder.

POCA: Don Amalio!

DON AMALIO: What's that?

POCA: Enedina and Paco…

DON AMALIO: What about them?

POCA: They're playing games behind the couch…

The blind man starts. His jaw trembles and anger takes hold of him. He seizes his stick and gets up.

DON AMALIO: Which couch?

POCA *(vaguely)* : That one.

Don Amalio puts his hand on Poca's shoulder.

DON AMALIO: Take me there.

POCA: Really, Don Amalio, there's not much point in making a fuss.

Poca, who does not seem to be too happy about this turn of events, walks toward the couch, followed by the blind man who is gripping him. Poca does not seem keen on getting involved in the events he stirred up and slithers out of the way, leaving his jacket in the hands of Amalio, whose fury is mounting.

DON AMALIO: Where are you, you swine? I'll crack your skull in. Take me to them and I'll kill him.

Without his guide he loses all sense of direction. He moves from one side to the other. In vain Hobbly tries to stop him. Overcome with rage the blind man clutches his cane and, facing the banquet table, lays about him with all his strength. His flaying creates havoc with the contents of the table: plates, glasses, bottles. Wines, sauces, and puddings are spilled. Very soon the beautiful embroidered tablecloth becomes a battlefield of destruction.

Paco and Enedina, terrified, get up from behind the couch.

Refugio and the gardener begin to be troubled by the turn of events. Disorderliness has turned into an orgy without anyone's really being aware of what is happening. A glimmer of sense in their befuddled minds makes the two women aware of the possible consequences.

In the middle of the room Enedina tidies herself up. The leper tries to extricate himself from the corset that he has wrapped himself in.

REFUGIO *(whispering to the gardener)* : Things are going to be worse than the Cuban War...

GARDENER: You're right. We'll be better off if we're seen in the village tonight.

They slip into the hall.

The blind man is finally in command. Don Zequiel falls face down and gets entangled in Doña Elvira's wedding veil as he tries in vain to stand up again.

LEPER: Now he has spoiled the party.

SINGER *(off)* : Holy Virgin, how can we fix up this brothel?

All of them have stopped dancing although the phonograph is still playing.

Enedina tries to justify herself.

ENEDINA *(apropos the blind man)* : If he were my man he'd have his rights; but as it is, why?

SINGER: You're quite right, old dear. The way he treats you...

Refugio and the gardener rush down the stairs into the lower hall. When they reach the big front door, they open it and go out into the park.

They have hardly left the building when they hear the noise of a car, and almost at once the headlights appear, making them hesitate for a moment and try to hide in the shadow. The music of Handel's Messiah is still playing.

The car rounds the turn in the road and comes to a halt in front of the house. Jorge, Ramona, then Viridiana and Rita get out one at a time. Viridiana, noting the two beggars running away, takes a few steps in their direction. Jorge realizes immediately that something abnormal has been going on. He sees a woman running away and hears the solemn chorus of Handel's Messiah. Without pausing a moment to reflect, he goes into the house.

The camera switches to the beggars grouped in the sitting room.

POCA: Now it's every man for himself. Let's go.

The camera shifts back to Jorge, entering the house. One by one the beggars pass him in the hall, looking crestfallen and as innocent as the situation allows. The first one he meets is Poca, who with great difficulty is support-

ing the almost completely unconscious Don Zequiel.

PACO: Good night... He doesn't feel too well.

Appalled, Jorge stands in the hall and watches the strange herd pass by. The singer, carrying one of the little girls, who is bawling, goes by with the dwarf.

SINGER: Good night, Don Jorge. We're leaving now...

Then it is Poca's and Enedina's turn. The latter has another infant in her arms.

ENEDINA *(pathetically)*: They told us you'd be back tomorrow...

POCA: I didn't want to do it, Don Jorge. They made me...

Jorge, quite beside himself, takes Poca by the arm.

JORGE: Get out of here! Out!

The blind man, led on as if by instinct and by the noise of the departing fugitives, goes toward the exit with the aid of his stick. He marches along, head high, his stick in front of him. It is difficult to know whether he is aware of Jorge's presence or not. On passing in front of him he intones in a sonorous voice.

DON AMALIO: Blessed are the generous, master, who take into their respectable house a poor defenseless blind man. God will reward them.

He advances while he speaks. His feet get entangled in the wedding veil which was left on the floor. Finally he gets rid of it with his stick and goes out as quickly as his blindness allows.

The room is now empty. Jorge, frowning, takes in the carnage caused by the senseless orgy. He advances toward the record player, where the Hallelujah Chorus is still playing, and turns it off. He starts suddenly on hearing the noise of furniture being knocked against in Don Jaime's room.

Jorge enters Don Jaime's room and gropes around in the half light. The room is faintly lit by one chandelier with the the six candles which are still intact. Jorge looks around. At first he does not see anybody. But then a curtain moves and he goes toward it.

JORGE *(shouting):* Didn't you hear me? Beat it. *(Hobbly appears from behind the curtain.)* Okay, get out, you.

Hobbly smiles in a sinister way.

HOBBLY: Your Lordship must not get annoyed: I have not done anything wrong...

Without saying a word Jorge advances on him, ready to seize his arm and put him out. Hobbly, now alert, suddenly pulls out a dagger. Jorge is undecided for a moment, but soon reacts by finding a chair in the passage and brandishing it, ready to attack his opponent. In a flash a raised arm behind him swings a bottle. Before he is aware of the danger, Jorge is hit by the bottle, staggers, and falls heavily to the floor. The leper, looking happy and proud of himself, leans over his victim.

LEPER: I got him, comrade. I got him!

At this point Viridiana appears at the door and is frightened by what she sees.

VIRIDIANA: My God, what have you done to him?

HOBBLY: He was asking for it.

VIRIDIANA: But why? Why? *(She rushes to him and leans over him, calling him in anguish.)* Jorge! Jorge!

Hobbly stops her and takes her by the arm.

HOBBLY: You shouldn't cry over that. If you're without one man you can always find another to console you.

He embraces her, crushing her cheek with his lips. She screams and looks around for a means of escape. She sees the leper and there is a glimmer of hope in her eyes.

VIRIDIANA: José, José! For the love of God, don't let him...

The leper empties a bottle and begins to jeer again without moving an inch.

LEPER: Nothing will happen to you, miss. We're all good folk here. Aren't we, Hobbly?

It is apparent from Viridiana's expression that she feels lost. She tries to escape but Hobbly takes hold of her again. She looks at him in terror.

Outside, in the park, the beggars have disappeared except for the old man Don Zequiel, who is staggering along the wall, helped by Paco. Ramona and her daughter are standing in front of the car and have seen them coming out of the house. So has the driver. Ramona makes up her mind and quickly gets back into the car with Rita.

RAMONA *(to the driver)* : To the village! We've got to warn...

DRIVER: They'll get them in no time. If they've stolen anything it won't do them any good.

The car starts up and moves quickly away from the estate.

Back in Don Jaime's room. Jorge is stretched out unconscious. The leper, kneeling, is tying up his legs with a curtain cord. He ties one end to the wardrobe.

HOBBLY *(off)* : Why all the fuss? It had to happen sooner or later!

VIRIDIANA: Ramona! Help!

They can be heard struggling. A chair crashes to the ground. The leper finishes tying up Jorge. His livid face looks ghostly in the half light. He laughs, jerking his head back as if he is having a fit of St. Vitus' dance. His work finished, he gets up and with the look of an impartial spectator watches the struggle between his benefactress and the beggar.

Viridiana is defending herself with more energy than she ever looked capable of. Hobbly is strong, but despair provides the young woman with equal strength. Hobbly pushes her onto the bed and then jumps on her, but Viridiana reacts quickly and flees toward the door. But the leper is waiting for her there and blocks her passage with folded arms. Hobbly catches his prey again and, holding her tightly in his arms, takes her once again to the bed.

VIRIDIANA *(screaming)* : Ramona! Ramona!

HOBBLY *(between his teeth, with rage)* : Quiet, my dove. Quiet, or
I'll...

*Jorge opens his eyes and, only half conscious, becomes aware of the struggle.
He desperately tries to free himself from his bonds but they do not give way.
With muffled voice he calls to the leper.*

JORGE: Come here! *(The leper jeers foolishly.)* Come her, you
rogue! Come here!

*The leper goes up to him and speaks in confidence, with a greedy laugh,
indicating the struggling couple.*

LEPER: Maybe afterwards he'll let me...

JORGE: If you free me you'll be a rich man...

The leper shrugs his shoulders, laughing.

LEPER: Me, rich? Come on!

JORGE: There's plenty of money in this house. Piles of it.

The leper becomes serious and leans a little lower in order to hear better.

LEPER: Where?

*Meanwhile, in the fight, Viridiana ends up by falling on the bed under
Hobbly. Her arms flail furiously in resistance. Her clenched hand grips
the cord that the beggar is using as a belt. It is Rita's jumprope, the same
one Don Jaime hanged himself with. As her hand touches the handle of the
rope, her gesture freezes. Then she lets go, dropping her arms as if giving
up the struggle. Hobbly brutally turns her face to his and avidly kisses her.*

But Jorge's words seem to have had an effect on the leper.

JORGE: I don't want you to untie me. Kill him and then I'll give
you the money.

LEPER: Where's the dough?

JORGE: Kill him and I'll tell you. If I don't keep my word you can kill me too. There are thousands of pesetas. Kill him, idiot!

The leper trembles with cupidity. He gets up, seizing an iron fire shovel. He goes toward the bed, where Viridiana seems to have fainted. Hobbly is embracing her. At this point the leper hits Hobbly's head with all his strength. There is the sound of heavy blows, then nothing more...

JORGE *(through clenched teeth)*: Kill him.

LEPER *(with a ferocious laugh)*: That will teach you not to bother me any more, you son of a bitch.

The leper, having satisfied his vengeance in order to gratify his avarice, turns to Jorge. Pointing the shovel at him, he reminds him savagely of his situation.

LEPER: Where's the cash?

Jorge realizes that the leper is quite likely to finish him off too. He is even more afraid that now that the leper is master of the house he might try to do something to Viridiana.

JORGE: There in the cupboard. It's open. *(The leper quickly opens the cupboard and begins looking.)* On the top shelf under the linen.

The leper looks there. He seizes piles of linen and throws them on the floor. Finally he finds a bundle of notes and counts them avidly.

Outside the house the car is back and stops in front of the door. Ramona and Rita get out, with the mayor and two policemen. They rush into the house. The driver is the last.

RAMONA: Up there.

MAYOR: Let's go!

The park, the next day. Two cows are being led toward the fields by the farmhand-coachman, who has returned. Rita is walking behind, playing with a stick and jumping happily in the grass. Old Moncho, who has also returned, is pushing the wheelbarrow beside them.

Inside the house Jorge stands near a door to one of the rooms with a man who is taking measurements and writing them down in a notebook.

JORGE: I want a switch here; and put a plug over there.

The man indicates the fitting on the other wall with chalk marks. He crosses the room. Jorge then turns to Viridiana, whose presence in the room is apparent only now. She is seated a few steps away sewing, dressed in a print blouse, which gives her an unexpectedly youthful air. She seems finally to have become just like any other young woman.

JORGE *(amiably but insistently)*: Have you got over the scare you had yesterday?

Viridiana, her eyes lowered, does not reply. Jorge turns around again and joins the man who was accompanying him. Their conversation continues, off.

JORGE: You can put the other plug there at the bottom for the two floor lamps that I've bought.

With her eyes Viridiana follows the young man who no longer pays any attention to her. It is a look we have never seen in her. It is undefinable, but seems full of gratitude, apology, and tenderness—a woman's look.

Viridiana's room, nighttime. Viridiana pulls out a small broken mirror from a drawer. By the light of a single candle she smooths her loose hair. She has cried and there are traces of tears on her cheeks. Without a doubt she is undergoing some internal struggle. She stands up, picks up a garment, and leaves.

On the drive near Viridiana's cell-like room, a brushwood fire has been lit. Moncho puts some leaves on it. It is cool and the old servant warms his hands over the flames and then goes off to find some more dry leaves.

Some jazz, in contrast with Handel's Messiah, begins to play. This continues until the end of the film.

Little Rita, her shoulders covered by the old blanket already seen on her, is sitting on a big stone near the fire. She is holding the crown of thorns dear

to Viridiana, looking at it curiously. While she is handling it she pricks her finger and a drop of blood appears. She sucks it, and after looking sorrowfully at the crown of thorns she throws it onto the fire with an air of detachment. The crown of thorns very soon becomes a crown of fire. Jazz music.

Don Jaime's room. Jorge with his sleeves rolled up is washing his hands and arms. Ramona is sitting on the edge of the turned-back bed sewing a button on Jorge's jacket. It is a peaceful family scene.

JORGE *(off)* : The towel.

Ramona puts the jacket on the bed and goes to look for the towel. She hands it to him. Jorge looks at her, smiling, while he is drying himself. He strokes her cheek. Ramona happily lets his hand run across her face to her mouth. She covers his hand with little kisses and nibbles it gently.

The jazz music gets louder; it is coming from the phonograph. The camera switches briefly to the crown of thorns in flames. With a stick, a hand takes it out of the flames and puts it on the ground, where it goes on burning and crackling.

In Don Jaime's room. Jorge and Ramona are startled by the noise of light rapid knocks on the door.

JORGE : Who's there?

Ramona starts to leave the room but Jorge stops her.

JORGE : Where are you going? Wait!

Nobody appears or replies and he goes to the door himself. Viridiana is there. Her expression is strange. She is apparenthy very calm but she betrays a great inner agitation. Her hair hangs loosely on her shoulders. She has never looked so feminine. Her appearance takes him by surprise.

JORGE : Come in, Viridiana. Has something happened?

She does not reply. She tries to look him in the eye but, overcome, soon lowers her gaze. She stands still and silent on the threshold.

JORGE : Did you want to speak to me? Is there anything I can do?

Jorge tries to penetrate her thoughts but does not succeed. Viridiana finally looks at him imploringly as if asking to be understood and pardoned. Jorge's concentrated gaze relaxes. As if by instinct he suddenly realizes that the long desired moment has arrived. The girl is at his mercy.

His smile is ironic but friendly as he moves back to let her in. Seeing Ramona there she is taken aback. Her face hardens and her body stiffens as she stares at the servant and then at Jorge. Ramona herself seems petrified, while Jorge, apparently at ease, tries to relax the atmosphere.

JORGE: I must say I was not expecting you. We are playing cards...

While he is talking he moves toward the table.

JORGE: I hope you are not surprised by this pastime, but the evenings are long and they must be got through, somehow. But... do sit down...

Viridiana, who is a little reassured, but not completely at home, taut, with a fixed look and without a word, follows him. Ramona, who feels she is not wanted, is about to leave.

JORGE: Don't leave, Ramona. Come here! Mademoiselle is not proud and she doesn't mind your staying here. Isn't that so?

Ramona goes timorously to the table. Viridiana's expression is blank. Jorge takes up the cards and shuffles them rigorously. He does not seem to find the situation at all unnatural.

JORGE: You know how to play cards, cousin? No? Then sit down. I'm sure you'll like it.

Viridiana, still detached, decides to sit down. Ramona remains standing, partly out of distress and partly out of respect.

JORGE: You too, sit down. Come on, sit down. All cats are gray at night...

Ramona sits down and Jorge finishes shuffling the cards.

JORGE: Do you like this music, Viridiana? It's popular now.

He puts the cards on the table in front of Viridiana. She is still taut and silent.

JORGE: Cut. Like that...

Close-up of Jorge's hand, which quietly takes Viridiana's limp hand and puts it on the cards, helping her with a light pressure to divide the pack. Jorge then puts the cards together and begins dealing to each according to the rules of the game...

JORGE: You won't believe me, but the first time I met you I said to myself: "My cousin Viridiana will end up playing cards with me."

He finishes dealing. Ramona is slightly animated. Viridiana, who seems to be paying no attention to what she is doing, with the tips of her fingers starts playing her cards.

The camera now recedes at top speed, showing the room in immense perspective. At the end of it the three players are soon almost indistinct in the center of the image. The shooting angle widens more and more and in the center of the image, while the music continues its euphoric and frenzied rhythm, there appear the words THE END.

The Exterminating Angel *(1962)*

Translated by Carol Martin-Sperry

Credits

Produced by Uninci and Films 59 (Gustavo Alatriste). Script and dialogue by Luis Buñuel from a story by Buñuel and Luis Alcoriza, suggested by an unpublished play by José Bergamin. Photographed by Gabriel Figueroa. Edited by Carlos Savage. Décor by Jesús Bracho.

Cast

Silvia Pinal	*Letitia (the "Valkyrie")*
Enrique Rabal	*Nobile*
Jacqueline Andere	*Alicia (Mrs. Roc)*
José Baviere	*Leandro*
Augusto Benedico	*The Doctor*
Luis Beristein	*Christian*
Antonio Bravo	*Russell*
Claudio Brook	*Butler*
Cesar del Campo	*The Colonel*
Rosa Elena Durgel	*Silvia*
Lucy Gallardo	*Lucia (Mrs. Nobile)*
Enrique Garcia Alvarez	*Mr. Roc*
Ofelia Guilmain	*Juana Avila*
Xavier Loya	*Francisco Avila*
Nadia Haro Oliva	*Ana Maynar*
Tito Junco	*Raul*
Xavier Masse	*Eduardo*

Ofelia Montesco	*Beatrice*
Angel Merino	*Waiter*
Patricia Moran	*Rita (Christian's wife)*
Bertha Moss	*Leonora*
Patricia de Morelos	*Blanca*

The credits, accompanied by a choral Te Deum, are shown over a shot of the cathedral at night. The camera moves down from the top of the façade to the entrance.

Boulevard in the town, nighttime. Close-up of a street sign: Calle de la Providencia. In the background, luxurious cars move along the road. It is apparent, in spite of the darkness, that the area is a wealthy one.

The large wrought-iron gate of a private estate. A man, followed by another man in livery. The first one to speak, who seems to be the major domo or butler, is holding the other back by his sleeve.

BUTLER: Hey! Where are you going?

LUCAS: I'm going for a little walk... not for long...

BUTLER: We've got twenty people coming to dinner... and you're going for a walk?

LUCAS *(embarrassed)*: I hadn't thought of that. But I'll be back as quickly as possible, I promise you.

Lucas wants to continue on his way out but the butler is still holding him back.

BUTLER: You shall not go!

LUCAS *(pleading)*: Please... please let me go...

BUTLER: All right, fine. Go. But don't ever set foot in this house again.

Lucas leaves, and the butler gives him a mean look and goes back in. The door closes behind him.

The drawing room. A valet picks up a pair of candelabra and crosses the drawing room to the dining room, where another valet is seen carrying a candlestick to the large dining table which has been set for dinner. The butler enters from a door at the end of the room and the first valet, holding the candelabra, enters from another side of the room. The butler inspects the table while he talks to the valets.

BUTLER: Lucas has quit... What got into him? Did he have a fight with you?

VALET I: No, not with us. He didn't even tell us he was leaving.

VALET II: We got along very well. He was a good man.

BUTLER: Oh well, if he didn't like it here he was right to leave... There are plenty of Lucases in the world!

VALET II *(shrugging his shoulders)*: Something to do with a woman, perhaps...

One of the valets leaves the room.

The kitchen. In the foreground, the chef's assistant is opening oysters in front of a table covered with food (lobster, caviar). An almost life-size glass swan is to serve as the caviar dish. Pablo, the chef, is in the background to the left. A maid passes through the kitchen carrying a tray of glasses. Another maid is wiping glasses.

MENI: Camila!

CAMILA: Yes?

MENI: What shall we do?

CAMILA: Whatever you want, but I can't tell you how much I want to get out. I can hardly contain myself.

MENI: Same here. But where can we go at this time of night?

CAMILA: Yes, it's late, and it's stormy.

Meni is pacing up and down the kitchen.

MENI: We could go and sleep at one of my friends' houses.

The chef's assistant comes over to them.

CHEF'S ASSISTANT: I'll come with you. I'll take you anywhere you want in a taxi. I've got to get one anyway.

While the chef's assistant is speaking, the chef, Pablo, who has been listening curiously, breaks in angrily.

PABLO: You! You're staying right here. *(Severely)* And you'll wait for me.

The two maids move away. Meni takes off her cap and apron. Camila does likewise. They go out toward the pantry. The Chef meanwhile is seeing to a dish that is cooking in the oven. Valet II comes in.

VALET II: Haven't you served the caviar yet?

PABLO: No, it comes after. Madam wants the ragout to be served first.

VALET I *(amazed)*: And I'm supposed to do it!

VALET II *(interrupting)*: Yes, because you're a fool!

Valet II tastes the dish and frowns.

Outside the mansion. Several cars come through the gate, drive around the forecourt, and stop in front of the steps. Guests get out of the cars and go up the steps.

The kitchen. The two maids enter and cross the room, putting on their hats and coats. It appears from their expressions that they are deliberately walking out. Close-up of the chef, who is astonished.

The two maids cross the hall but stop suddenly when they hear the voices of the arriving guests. They go back and hide in a closet near a column of the huge staircase. A group of guests comes in through the front door. They are all in dinner jackets and long evening dresses. The host, Nobile, comes forward from the group, looking for a valet.

NOBILE *(calling)*: Lucas! That's strange. Lucas isn't there. *(He returns to his guests and shows them upstairs.)* We'll get rid of our coats upstairs. Come up, come up, please.

The camera returns to the maids in the closet.

MENI: Can you hear anything?

CAMILA: They must be upstairs by now.

MENI: Walking out like this... it's not right...

CAMILA: You should have thought of that before. You can stay, you know!

MENI: Let's go!

They run toward the door, then rush back to their hiding place (same shot as before). New shot of the front door and repeat of the guests' entrance as it was seen before. Nobile (seen this time from a higher angle) comes forward from his guests, looking for a valet.

NOBILE *(calling)*: Lucas? *(He returns to his guests and shows them the staircase.)* That's strange! Lucas isn't there. We'll get rid of our coats upstairs. Come up, come up, please.

The two maids come out of the closet again and go down the front steps as the last couple comes up.

The kitchen. The chef, standing with his assistant, puts the caviar in the glass swan.

The dining room. The butler hands over a bottle of champagne to a valet. The valet takes it to the table where the guests are seated.

A GUEST *(off)*: No, I've never eaten it before.

BLANCA: So, although you're the youngest colonel in the army, you've never aspired to honor and glory?

COLONEL: I can't stand the noise of the cannons, Blanca.

BLANCA: But... what about your country?

COLONEL: My country is a multitude of rivers that flow into the sea.

BLANCA: The sea—which is Death!

COLONEL: There you are! To die for one's country.

Lucia, the mistress of the house, is seated at the end of the table beyond the colonel. She discreetly takes hold of the colonel's hand and looks in front of her toward her husband, Nobile, who is sitting at the head of the table.

LUCIA: I think my husband wants to say something.

Nobile stands up with his glass in his hand.

NOBILE: Here's to the wonderful evening that Silvia gave us... with her magnificent interpretation of the virgin fiancée in "Lammermoor."

Silvia smiles. The young Francisco and the doctor are on either side of her. She lowers her eyes and thanks him with a movement of her head. All the guests drink.

LEANDRO *(ironically)* : Fiancée, perhaps... but virgin!

ANA MAYNAR : Virginity would suit the Valkyrie better...

The "Valkyrie" (Letitia) is seen unfolding her napkin while the preceding conversation continues off screen.

LEANDRO *(off)* : The Valkyrie?

ANA *(off, then the camera returns to them both)* : Yes, Letitia. I call her that because she is wild... and a virgin.

Pause. Short, quick close-up of Ana looking pensively toward Letitia.

LEANDRO : A virgin? Do you think so?

ANA : They say she's still kept it. *(Pensively)* Maybe it's some perversion...

The camera returns to Nobile, who stands up again with his glass in his hand and repeats his toast.

NOBILE : Here's to the wonderful evening Silvia gave us... with her magnificent interpretation of the virgin fiancée in "Lammermoor." *He sits down in confusion, realizing that no one is listening to him. At the other end of the table, Lucia speaks.*

LUCIA : Forgive me if I change the order of the menu. We shall start with a Maltese dish. According to the customs of the land, this is served as an hors d'œuvre because it sharpens the appetite. Liver! Honey! Almonds! And an enormous amount of spices in the sauce!

MR. ROC : Delicious! I had some in Capri once, during a concert I was conducting there...

Lucia who looks around toward the pantry door: the butler lets through a valet carrying a large dish.

MR. ROC: How theatrical! Here it is!

The valet comes toward the camera, trips and falls (a trick arranged by Lucia). Close-up of the dish falling and food and sauce scattered everywhere. The surprised guests wipe themselves off; some are laughing; others are complaining somewhat, especially a certain Mr. Russell. The valet, pretending to be shamefaced, wipes himself off and leaves the room. The guests sit down again and make various comments.

RAUL: Delicious, Lucia! Quite unexpected.

BLANCA: Lucia really has a flair for that kind of surprise!

RUSSELL: I didn't find it the slightest bit funny.

Lucia stands up worriedly. She goes toward the pantry door and makes a friendly and reassuring sign to her husband, who seems embarrassed and ill at ease. She walks into the pantry and goes up to the butler.

LUCIA *(severely)*: I've come just in time.

The camera shows a bear growling in the room (a brown bear that Lucia will use for another trick).

LUCIA *(off)*: Don't let it out. Mr. Russell doesn't like practical jokes. Take it into the garden.

BUTLER *(a little tight-lipped)*: Madam's decision reassures me... there are important matters for her to attend to.

LUCIA: What's happening?

BUTLER: Strange things. *(He bids her lean over to take a closer look.)* If Madam would come with me... *(Close-up of a flock of sheep under the table.)* And the sheep, madam?

The two of them face each other.

LUCIA *(very sure of herself)*: Also in the garden.

Shot of the bear frisking and turning a somersault.

The kitchen. The chef and his assistant come in through the service door;

they cross the kitchen, dressing to go out, just as the maids had done. They hear Lucia's voice, off. The chef's assistant immediately takes off his raincoat; the chef removes his hat obsequiously.

LUCIA *(off)* : Where are you going?

The two men come back. They are very ill at ease and do not quite know what to do. The butler is in the background.

PABLO *(trembling)* : Madam...

LUCIA : What does this mean, Pablo? Are you going?

PABLO *(eagerly)* : Well... yes, madam. I'm hurrying to see my sister. Poor thing...

LUCIA : What's happened to your sister? Is she ill?

PABLO : This morning she wasn't feeling very well, and I'm afraid that now...

LUCIA : I can't believe it! What an insult! How dare you leave when my guests have just sat down to dinner?

PABLO : Madam will please excuse us, but everything is ready.

LUCIA : But... what is it? Aren't you happy here?

PABLO : Oh, indeed, madam. I have spent five years in Madam's service—years which I remember most warmly.

LUCIA : So?

PABLO : I beg of Madam to excuse me.

His embarrassed assistant leaves the frame. Lucia turns around quickly and goes toward him.

LUCIA : And you? Where are you going?

CHEF'S ASSISTANT : I'm going with Mr. Pablo *(pointing at him)*. We'll be back tomorrow morning—very early.

LUCIA : Don't trouble yourselves. If you go now you can consider yourselves dismissed.

PABLO *(embarrassed)* : I would like to be of service to Madam, but... I beg you to excuse us... with your permission...

The chef passes in front of Lucia, nods, and goes out. Lucia turns to the butler.

LUCIA: I'm quite sure they're in this together... But why? Oh, well...

BUTLER: Servants are becoming more and more disrespectful.

LUCIA *(leaving the kitchen)* : Well, carry on with the valets. I'm counting on you.

They go out. The two valets come through the pantry door dressed and ready to go out. In the hall one of them pours himself a glass of champagne and drinks it.

VALET II: We'll have to take our things with us.

VALET I: Not now. Let's go right away. We can come back and get our things tomorrow.

VALET II: Tomorrow?... They won't even let us in. I'll pack my bags very quickly. Wait for me outside.

Valet II goes back toward the pantry to get his belongings while the other pours himself a glass of champagne and drinks.

The dining room. Letitia (the "Valkyrie") is sitting alone at the table, folding her napkin. Piano music is heard coming from the next room. She stands up, picks up an ash tray from the table, and throws it violently at the window. The windowpane breaks noisily.

The drawing room. Two of the guests, Leandro and Raul, turn around at the sound of the breaking glass. In the background the other guests pause.

LEANDRO *(looking scornfully at the window)* : A Jew going by!

RAUL: No, it was the Valkyrie!

LEANDRO: What an enchanting woman!

Some of the guests are dancing in the drawing room. The Valkyrie walks haughtily past Leandro and Raul. A couple talk as they dance.

EDUARDO: What's your name?

BEATRICE: Beatrice—and yours?

EDUARDO: Eduardo.

BEATRICE: Age?

EDUARDO: 30.

They pause, look at each other, then start dancing again.

BEATRICE: Profession?

EDUARDO: Architect.

BEATRICE: Single?

EDUARDO: Till Saturday, like you.

BEATRICE: Five more days!

She clings to him very passionately and they continue dancing. The camera shows another group: the doctor, standing; near him, Leonora, in front of a table, finishing a cup of coffee; in the background, the butler. Leonora goes up to the doctor seductively and holds out her empty cup to him, which he gives to the butler.

LEONORA: I feel marvelously well. My appetite was very good tonight, doctor. Your treatment has really changed me.

DOCTOR: I don't deserve any credit... There was nothing seriously wrong with you.

LEONORA: Do you dance, doctor?

DOCTOR: I've never tried.

LEONORA: Pity! *(Leaning against him)* I would love to be in your arms...

They begin to walk.

DOCTOR: I'm flattered that my patient should feel so warmly about me, but... *(Leonora interrupts him and suddenly kisses him on the mouth. A pause; then the doctor sighs to himself.)* Transference!

LEONORA: I've been wanting to fulfill that wish for a long time!

The camera turns to Christian and Rita.

RITA *(in a low voice, but firmly, to her husband, Christian)*: Did you bring your pills?

As he nods, the doctor comes up behind them.

DOCTOR: What is it?

RITA: It's nothing, doctor. *(To Christian)* I warned you: "Don't eat too much, Christian." *(Turning toward the doctor for support)* An ulcer doesn't make allowances.

Raul joins the group, bringing his friend Leandro with him.

RAUL *(to Christian)*: May I introduce you to a good friend of mine, who has just arrived in our town. Leandro Gomez—Christian Galvez.

LEANDRO *(a little coldly)*: How do you do.

The two men shake hands at great length. Behind these five guests, Russell is loitering and eavesdropping.

CHRISTIAN *(to Leandro)*: How do you do. *(The two men look at each other for a moment, and then Christian draws away.)* Excuse me.

Raul nods and moves away himself, taking the doctor by the arm.

RAUL: But of course... Doctor...

Leonora passes them quickly.

LEONORA: Aren't you coming to listen to Blanca?

RAUL: Right away... we're coming right away. *(To the doctor, in a low voice)* Why did she kiss you so passionately? *(Close-up of the two men. The doctor shrugs his shoulders.)* Poor Leonora. *(Pause)* And how is the cancer progressing? Is there any hope?

DOCTOR: None whatsoever. I give her just three months to lose all her hair and drop dead.

RAUL: Oh, but she's in top condition!

The camera shifts to Christian, standing alone. He takes a pill. The butler steps forward at once and offers him a glass of water on a tray. He drinks, puts the glass back on the tray, turns around and goes toward Leandro.

CHRISTIAN *(exclaiming)*: Leandro!

LEANDRO *(opening his arms)*: My dear friend! Christian!

CHRISTIAN: How wonderful! I thought you were still in New York!

LEANDRO: Well! As you can see, one must have courage in the face of adversity.

CHRISTIAN: We must see a lot of each other!

LEANDRO: But of course! You must come around tomorrow. I have a present for you.

Russell passes behind them, still prying and eavesdropping.

CHRISTIAN *(low)*: Be careful, we are not alone. *(He goes toward Russell.)* Let me introduce you to Mr. Russell.

RUSSELL *(sarcastically)*: Don't worry! Carry on, carry on with your introductions. In any case I don't understand Greek. Excuse me...

He moves away.

CHRISTIAN *(haughtily)*: Russell is somewhat eccentric.

LEANDRO: He must be a man of letters. That's too bad!

Christian's wife, Rita, arrives.

RITA: Suppose we go into the drawing room to listen to Blanca... what do you think?

Christian offers Rita his arm and together they go toward the drawing room.

The drawing room. Blanca is playing a grand piano on a platform. Letitia is standing, leaning on the piano. The colonel is seated in the foreground, listening attentively. He discreetly looks at his watch. The doctor is standing alone, listening attentively; Nobile is also standing. All the other guests are seated as if they were at a performance. In the foreground Raul stifles a yawn.

The recital continues. The camera moves around the audience and stops on Christian. He is standing, trying to catch the eye of someone in the audience.

Finally, when he has found him, he makes the Masonic sign of recognition. The camera rapidly follows the direction of his gaze to Mr. Roc, the old conductor, seated in the audience. The latter replies very discreetly by giving the same sign.

Ana Maynar is sitting next to Lucia. Ana puts her handbag on her lap and opens it. She takes two chicken claws out of her bag and then a handkerchief, which she raises to her face.

Blanca finishes a Paradisi sonata. She stands up, looking tired. The colonel rushes up at once to congratulate her, as does Letitia. Gradually they all surround her and praise her.

NOBILE: The recital would have been excellent with a harpsichord.

RAUL: Something by Scarlatti now, Blanca, I implore you.

BLANCA *(drawing back a little):* Please excuse me... It's late and I'm tired.

NOBILE: Late? But this is the most intimate and pleasant moment of the night.

In a corner of the drawing room, Christian goes up to Roc, to whom he had previously made the sign. The latter stands up at once and comes toward him.

CHRISTIAN: So, the world-famous conductor is one of us? Who would have thought it?

MR. ROC: I'm very pleased to know you in such a... brotherly way.

CHRISTIAN: What lodge?

MR. ROC *(in a low voice):* Dawn Twenty-one.

CHRISTIAN: Sublime Column.

Roc puts his hand on his chest and starts to make a sign, when they are interrupted by Leandro, who comes up behind them.

LEANDRO: What do you think of the pizzicato we just heard, sir?

MR. ROC *(correcting him):* The sonata, sir, sonata. Let me introduce you. Mr. Ugalde... and your name, please?

LEANDRO: Leandro Gomez. How do you do.

Roc sits down.

CHRISTIAN: How do you do! Are you staying with us for long?

LEANDRO: What about you?

CHRISTIAN: No, you first!

LEANDRO: No, you! As for me, I live here.

CHRISTIAN *(ironically):* I might have known.

Leandro withdraws. As he comes up to the Valkyrie and Russell, the latter takes his arm. He is very surprised at the preceding dialogue, which he tried to overhear.

Nobile, who is standing by the door that separates the big drawing room from the smaller drawing room, calls the butler.

NOBILE: Julio, could you see to the cloakroom?

BUTLER: Yes, sir!

The butler nods and departs. Nobile turns around. The camera follows his look to the couch, where Roc is sprawled out, apparently asleep. His wife, Alicia, is loosening his tie. Nobile comes up to them, looking surprised.

ALICIA: You must forgive him. Tonight he feels young again. He had a little to drink and... drink and exhaustion...

Alicia sits down next to Roc and looks at him as though he were a child, while Nobile leans over him.

NOBILE: Alberto's stamina is wonderful. You only have to see him conduct... I don't know how he can stand two hours of great tension... and other activities as well...

Nobile sits down next to Alicia.

ALICIA *(almost confidentially)*: Well, when we retired to rest after the concert, he tried again. I can't complain from that point of view—on the contrary, I have to hold him back.

NOBILE: Let him sleep... he could try again here.

ALICIA: My God, no! I don't think he would dare here.

NOBILE: No, of course not... I expressed myself rather badly.

The camera shifts to Christian, supporting his wife Rita. He leads her to another couch, where she lies down. Some guests come up, with Lucia, the mistress of the house, and Juana.

CHRISTIAN: It's nothing. She's feeling a bit tired. In her condition, it's to be expected.

LUCIA: It's a good sign that she's sleepy. Congratulations!

CHRISTIAN: Thank you.

LUCIA: It's your fourth child, isn't it?

CHRISTIAN: I don't know. I can't keep count any more.

JUANA: Are you sure you know who the father is? I mean...

CHRISTIAN: You'd better ask her.

RITA *(tired)*: Science will tell.

Lucia leaves them and goes up to another group consisting of Blanca, Ana, and Raul.

LUCIA: Blanca! I thought you'd gone.

BLANCA: I stayed on for a little. Raul was explaining to us that the fauna in Rumania...

RAUL: Because of the harshness of the climate...

BLANCA: But we've been chatting too long. I'm really going. *(She touches her shoulders.)* Where did I put my shawl?

LUCIA: Just a moment.

Lucia leaves the group, passes in front of the colonel, and pauses. He looks impatiently at his watch. Lucia continues on her way, lifts the curtain that hides the cloakroom, and takes Blanca's shawl. The colonel comes up, pushes back the curtain, and leans right up against her. They kiss each other passionately. He draws back.

COLONEL *(worried)*: How come they're not leaving? It's nearly four o'clock.

LUCIA: They'll go in a few minutes. Take advantage of the general confusion to slip into my boudoir.

COLONEL: What about your husband?

LUCIA: If he comes I'll tell him I wanted to show you my historical print.

COLONEL: What a good idea!

The camera shifts to Leandro, who yawns and then undoes his tie and puts it on a chair. Lucia gives Blanca her shawl. In the foreground, Francisco is sleeping. His sister, Juana, watches over him lovingly.

BLANCA *(to Lucia):* Thank you very much.

Lucia goes and sits down next to her husband.

NOBILE: Everything went very well, Lucia, in spite of... *(He wipes a smear of lipstick from her mouth.)* It's late and your lipstick is wearing off. *(She starts anxiously.)* The problem now is to look after our friends. They must feel a little awkward. *(While he talks, without looking at her, Lucia takes out a mirror and fixes her lipstick.)* I like the unpredictable quality of this situation. *(Nobile stands up, switches off a lamp near by, and goes up to Christian who is stifling a yawn.)* If you'd like to spend the night here, we can make beds for you all. I'm glad to see that the good old spirit of improvisation is still alive.

COLONEL *(to Nobile):* You're the perfect host, Edmundo. *(Pause)* But personnally I dont't want to make any unnecessary demands on your generous hospitality.

They all agree.

SILVIA: Unfortunately, I have to go to a show tomorrow afternoon, and...

CHRISTIAN: And I have an appointment early tomorrow morning... *(Looks at his watch)* That is to say, in four hours.

He leaves the scene. The camera shifts to the butler in the small drawing room. He looks toward the large drawing room: one by one the guests pass in front of the open double doors that divide the two rooms. None of them crosses the threshold. The butler, who is a little tired, turns out the lights in the small drawing room. In the large drawing room the colonel comes up to the doctor and Russell, who are slightly in the shadows.

DOCTOR: Hey, it looks serious. They're turning off the lights!

RUSSELL: The time has come to make a decision. We should leave this very moment. If the others are drunk or have all gone crazy, well, let them stay.

Behind the colonel Leandro is seen taking off his jacket. The colonel stares at him in dismay.

COLONEL: But... *(Almost stammering)* But it's incredible! *(In the background, Leandro is undoing his tie.)* If only for the respect that I owe my host I'd like to teach that boor a lesson!

Leandro passes in front of Christian, who is lying on a couch next to his wife.

LEANDRO: These stiff clothes are fine for statues but not for men... especially at five in the morning.

Christian lifts up his head and looks at Leandro, who stretches himself out on the floor. Christian stands up and takes off his jacket too. The camera comes back to Lucia and Nobile.

LUCIA: They're taking off their dinner jackets! Don't you think that's a bit much?

NOBILE: Don't forget that Leandro lived in the United States. And at such a late hour bodies reach the limit of exhaustion. *(Pause)* And the temperature in here is so pleasant.

LUCIA: I'm sure they'll feel ashamed when they remember their behavior.

NOBILE: So am I, I'd hate them to feel embarrassed. *(He takes off his own jacket.)* Let's come down to their level so as to mitigate their bad manners.

The camera turns to Ana, who settles down in an armchair, ready to sleep. Leandro is lying on the floor. In the small drawing room the butler takes off his jacket, sits down near the center table, blows out the candles, drinks from a nearby glass, and falls asleep with his head on the table. The room is in semi-darkness. In the large drawing room Lucia's husband lies down on the floor. She watches him, then crosses the room, passes in front of the colonel, and sits down next to Christian, who stands up at once, very politely.

CHRISTIAN: Please, Lucia, take my place.

Christian, after giving his place to Lucia, lies down on the floor. The camera moves to the lovers, sitting very close to each other. They stand up and move away a little. Close-up of them in the darkness.

EDUARDO: Our first night together.

BEATRICE: But what are we doing here? Why haven't we left?

They embrace. Close-up of Eduardo's hands on Beatrice's breasts.

EDUARDO: But everyone has decided to stay.

BEATRICE: Do you think that's normal?

EDUARDO: Life is funny... and strange.

Close-up of Eduardo's hands caressing Beatrice's thighs and buttocks.

BEATRICE: I can hardly keep on my feet.

EDUARDO: Come on. *(He takes her toward the piano.)* Let's go and sleep.

Eduardo and Beatrice lie down. He undoes his tie. The colonel passes.

Russell is pacing up and down in front of the entrance to the big drawing room. He looks up in the air, seems worried, and without attempting to cross the threshold, goes back to the middle of the room and sits down in a chair. He takes off his glasses and, somewhat intrigued and pensive, looks all around him. He seems very tired and, putting his hand on his heart, appears to be suffering silently.

Quick exterior shot: general view of the boulevard at dawn, then of the Nobile mansion.

The small drawing room. The butler, in his shirt sleeves, combs his hair in front of a large mirror, fixes his tie, and puts on his jacket. In the background, the guests in the big drawing room are awakening and beginning to get up.

Silvia, Rita, and Ana scrutinize each other with embarrassment, because of their attire, and with affection, because of a certain ambiguity surrounding each of them.

SILVIA: Good morning, Rita. Did you sleep well?

RITA: You won't believe it, but I slept straight through.

ANA: I, on the other hand... *(Stretching)* What a night. Even after the train crash at Nice I never felt so stiff.

RITA: You've been in a train crash? How exciting!

SILVIA *(to Ana):* If you could see yourself in the mirror!

Another corner of the drawing room. Lucia is arranging her hair in front of a mirror. Nobile comes up to her.

NOBILE: I'm confused. *(Looking around him)* What's happening here? I can't think how it ever came to this. *(Pause)* But everything has to come to an end.

LUCIA: I don't know what to say to you. For the moment, I think we must offer them breakfast. After that they're bound to go home.

NOBILE: I hope so. *(Pause)* And I'm counting on their discretion.

Ana is still telling the story of "her" accident to Silvia and Rita.

ANA: I was going from one corner to another, like a madwoman. The third-class compartment, full of common people, had been squashed like a huge accordion. And inside... what carnage! I must be insensitive, because the suffering of those poor people didn't move me at all.

The Valkyrie (Letitia) comes in.

LETITIA: I'm hungry.

SILVIA: Insensitive? And yet you fainted at the lying-in-state of Prince Luttar.

ANA: Oh! How could you make such a comparison? How could one be insensitive before the grandeur of the death... of that admirable prince, who was our friend... And such a noble profile...

LETITIA *(insisting)*: Don't they eat breakfast in this house?

RITA *(Quick close-up)*: Well, I think that the common people, the lower classes, are less sensitive to pain. Have you ever seen a wounded bull? Quite impassive!

SILVIA: Well, I'm going to tidy up a bit. We all look... horrible. *(Simpering)* But it's so amusing...

They separate. In another part of the drawing room, Francisco wakes up next to his older sister, Juana, who is still being very attentive.

JUANA *(at Francisco's first movement)*: Did you sleep well?

FRANCISCO *(feminine, haughty, theatrical)*: Why are you looking at me like that, dear sister? I must look awful.

Behind them the guests stretch and unbend.

JUANA *(lovingly)*: You're more interesting than ever. It suits you to be disheveled.

Francisco stands up and wanders around the drawing room. The camera follows him and stops on the seated lovers.

BEATRICE: Why are you looking at me like that? I must look awful.

Beatrice mechanically wipes Eduardo's mouth with her handkerchief.

EDUARDO: You're more interesting than ever. It suits you to be disheveled.

Francisco stands over them severely.

FRANCISCO: You have very sharp ears!

Close-up of Russell sleeping uneasily, with his collar open. The doctor comes toward him. He takes his pulse and then puts his ear to his heart. Other guests come up to the couch on which Russell is stretched out.

LETITIA: He had a very bad night. He lost consciousness at dawn. Then he recovered a little.

NOBILE: Why didn't you tell me right away? We must take him to a room and put him to bed.

DOCTOR *(standing up)* : At the moment it's better not to move him. We'll see what we can do for him. He mustn't catch cold.

LETITIA : Good.

The doctor stands up and moves away. The camera follows him to Leonora.

LEONORA : Even last night at dinner I thought he seemed a little strange.

SILVIA : It may not be anything serious. He's already had similar attacks.

LEONORA : How do you find him, doctor?

DOCTOR *(low)* : In a few hours he'll lose all his hair and...

LEONORA: I'm sorry. I don't understand.

DOCTOR *(low)*: I mean he has only a few hours to live.

LEONORA *(horrified)*: That's awful... because your diagnoses are never wrong. *(Pause)* I don't feel very well either. *(She moves toward him.)*

DOCTOR: Don't be silly.

Leonora takes hold of the doctor's hand and kisses it feverishly; he withdraws it.

Lucia walks toward the small drawing room, stops suddenly on the threshold without being able to go on, looks up and then down. The butler comes up from the direction of the small drawing room.

LUCIA: Julio, do the best you can, but I simply must have a good breakfast for my guests.

BUTLER: Excuse me, madam, but it's so early that the tradesmen haven't been here yet.

LUCIA: Not even the milkman?

BUTLER: No, not even he... and that's very strange!

LUCIA: There's some cold meat left over from dinner. Bring it in with some hot coffee.

She turns around and looks once more toward the doorway that separates the two rooms. The butler nods and goes. Lucia returns to the center of the drawing room. Rita and Ana come up to her.

RITA: Lucia, my dear, excuse me, but... where could we tidy ourselves up a bit?

LUCIA: Of course. Forgive me for not seeing to it earlier. Let's go to my boudoir.

The colonel follows the three women with his eyes as they go toward the small drawing room. He points them out to Raul, who is coming toward him.

COLONEL: I bet they won't go out. *(In the background the three women stop.)* You see? *(Eduardo comes up to the colonel; in the background the three women, rooted to the spot, seem to be just as embarrassed as they are worried.)* What do you say to this situation?

RAUL: Indeed, I don't know what to say. It seems most improbable. Unless, of course, it's only too normal.

EDUARDO: What worries me is that no one seems to be asking themselves any questions.

COLONEL: Why didn't you leave with your fiancée last night?

EDUARDO: Well, I don't know... Like everyone else... And you?

COLONEL: I can't say. *(Pause)* And that's what's worrying me. *(He seems to draw away and then come back.)* After the party last night, none of us made any effort whatsoever to leave. Why? Do you think it's normal to have spent the night here in this drawing room without showing any elementary signs of good manners? *(The colonel walks around the room; he passes in front of Ana, who is holding her handbag, ready to leave.)* Or to have turned the room into the most unbelievable gypsy camp?

ANA: Well, I found it all very original. I love anything that's an escape from routine.

Silvia comes up.

SILVIA: Well, I realized... and I didn't like it... I didn't say anything... out of politeness.

Leandro, who is alone, is sitting on a chair near the piano putting on his shoes.

LEANDRO: Come, come, gentlemen. We mustn't exaggerate. We were all thrilled. Music, stimulating conversation, good humor... One mustn't be surprised. *(He has trouble putting on his second shoe.)* My feet have swollen!

The doctor is standing in the middle of the room.

DOCTOR: Could our charming friend, Lucia, tell us why, for example, she told the butler to serve us breakfast in here instead of in the dining room?

The doctor turns around toward Lucia. She is standing on one side and the doctor, Rita, Christian, Letitia, and Juana on the other. Juana and the doctor are smoking.

LUCIA: Well, I don't know, doctor. As we were all here together, I thought...

RAUL *(interrupting)*: The doctor loves playing Sherlock Holmes. *(Turning toward Blanca)* Don't you agree?

BLANCA: I must go home. My husband and my children must be worried. I'm going immediately.

MR. ROC: Alicia and I will go with you. *(Shrugging his shoulders)* This is all we needed! The whole thing is absurd. Let's go.

He takes Alicia by the arm and accompanies Blanca to the entrance to the drawing room.

BLANCA: Are you coming, Rita?

RITA: Not yet. What can one do in the streets so early in the morning?

BLANCA: But my God, Rita, you also have children who go to school.

RITA: My children learn at home. They have a tutor—Father Samson. *(Simpering, almost flirtatious)* A very fine and cultivated man with beautiful manners. I believe, forgive me if I exaggerate, that he has the essential qualities of a saint. Even if my husband believes that... *(Pause)* Aren't I right, Christian?

MR. ROC *(irritated)*: But madam, this is no time to talk of priests! What does it have to do with us? *(Pushing Alicia)* Let's go.

They move forward, but the butler comes in from the small drawing room, pushing a cart of food. They stand aside to let him pass.

BUTLER: Excuse me...

The butler passes. Alicia and Roc confer.

MR. ROC: All things considered, what have we got to lose by drinking a cup of coffee? I don't like to smoke on an empty stomach.

ALICIA: I'd like some too. Are you coming with us, Blanca?

They both turn around, pass in front of Blanca, and go to the middle of the room. Blanca shakes her head as they go by. She paces up and down in front of the doorway that divides the two drawing rooms but does not cross the threshold. Finally she sits down by the entrance.

Letitia rushes up to the food cart. The other guests follow.

JUANA: I find this atmosphere of fear quite excessive—indeed, almost hysterical.

RAUL: This isn't the first time I've stayed till eight in the morning at a party like this one.

ALICIA: Excuse me, Lucia, but there are no small spoons for the sugar.

LUCIA: I'm the one who must be excused. Poor Julio is snowed under with work... Julio, could you bring the small spoons?

BUTLER: Yes, madam. *(The butler stops in front of the doorway between the two rooms, lifts his head and, with embarrassment, goes back to the colonel and the doctor.)* Do these gentlemen require anything? A cup of coffee? Some ham?

COLONEL: Nothing, Julio. Just do what was asked of you.

BUTLER *(very embarrassed)*: I think it would be better to wait for these ladies and gentlemen to finish their breakfast before I clear it away...

LUCIA *(interrupting)* : But what's happened to you, Julio? Didn't you hear me ask you to go get the small spoons?

BUTLER: I just thought I'd suggest to these gentlemen that...

LUCIA *(severely)* : That's enough. Please carry out my orders.

The butler bows to Lucia and goes back to the doorway between the two rooms. He stops and seems to be taken ill. He sits down on a nearby chair and slumps over. First Lucia and then the guests come up to him.

LUCIA: But what's happened to you? Aren't you feeling well?...

Lucia leans toward the butler, who looks at her without answering. Lucia turns around and goes to Blanca, who is also slumped in a chair. Blanca is crying. Lucia kneels down next to her, as though imploring her.

LUCIA: And you, Blanca? What's happened to you? Can I help you?

The colonel and the doctor stand to the side, watching.

COLONEL: What's your opinion of what has just happened?

DOCTOR: This strange resistance of the butler against carrying out orders confirms my observations. Since last night, not a single one of us, even had he tried to, has been able to leave this room. What's happening, my dear Aranda?

The colonel does not answer and moves away.

The front steps of the mansion. A dark night with heavy rain, lightning, and thunder. A window is fleetingly lit up by the storm.

The small drawing room. The camera slowly moves from the window, seen from the inside, to the doorway between the two rooms. Roc, looking up in the air, passes in front of the doorway, then Alicia, who seems very downcast, then Francisco. Someone is nervously playing the piano.

The drawing room. It is Blanca playing the piano, almost slumped over it. Letitia comes up and, with a sudden gesture, angrily slams down the piano lid.

LETITIA: There's a very sick man here!

Blanca does not reply. Letitia comes down from the platform, quite unruffled.

Russell, his collar open, is breathing with difficulty. The doctor is leaning over him and examing him worriedly. The doctor stands up and wearily walks away from the sick man. Roc comes up to him.

MR. ROC: How is he, doctor?

DOCTOR: I don't see why I should hide the truth: he's in a coma. If only I had at least some coramine or some camphorated oil. *(Turning toward Christian)* Please, we must get Mr. Russell out of here and take him somewhere where he can be treated properly as quickly as possible.

CHRISTIAN: Dr. Conde is right. *(To Raul and Francisco)* We must make an effort! Which of you dares to take him?

RAUL: And why won't you do it yourself? Then we'll all follow you, you'll see!

FRANCISCO: It's useless! *(He woefully goes up to his sister, Juana, and sits down next to her. Lucia is listening attentively near them.)* We're finished. *(Severely, to his sister)* Why did you bring me here, my dear sister, why?

He is almost shouting. The excited guests come toward Francisco. In another corner of the drawing room, Letitia discreetly goes up to a closet in the wall, decorated with a virgin and child, opens it, takes the key and puts it in the inside of the door. She goes into the closet, which is full of Chinese vases, and locks herself in. Beatrice walks up to the food cart. The butler is standing still next to it, looking tired. Beatrice takes an empty carafe, turns it upside down, and shrugs her shoulders.

BEATRICE: There's no water left... but coffee perhaps. *(Pleading)* A little coffee, please... I'm dying of thirst.

Eduardo passes behind them and goes toward a flower vase.

BUTLER *(humble):* I'm very sorry, madam, but... there isn't a drop left...

While he is speaking, Eduardo, who is still behind them, takes the flowers out of the vase and throws them on the floor. He offers Beatrice the vase full of water.

EDUARDO: This water doesn't smell too good, but it can't be bad. *(He squeezes a lemon over the vase.)* A little lemon will remove the bad taste.

BEATRICE *(a little disgusted)*: No, thank you, Eduardo, I'd rather wait.

Eduardo, disappointed, puts down the vase. Meanwhile Raul is walking around in the center of the drawing room, speaking to them all.

RAUL: I really don't understand. There must be a solution. Look at me closely. We haven't gone crazy, have we?

BLANCA: We've already been here twenty-four hours and nobody has come. They've forgotten us.

MR. ROC: The attitude of the people outside worries me more than our own situation. What's happened to them? They should have tried something.

COLONEL: Unless everyone in town has died and we are the last survivors.

A woman cries out. It is Leonora, who is sitting down, supported by Rita and Christian.

LEONORA *(her eyes wide)*: Why don't they come and get us?

RITA: Keep calm now, keep calm, don't lose your head.

They all come up to comfort her. Various shouts, arguments. Leonora appears to be hysterical.

LETITIA: I'm going to break a window.

RAUL: What for? The door's over there.

Roc goes up to Nobile threateningly. Christian and Raul are behind them.

MR. ROC: It's connected with the servants' leaving. Why did they go?

NOBILE: Please, gentlemen. You mustn't jump to such alarming conclusions. *(Not knowing what to say)* Er... the servants... er... had their reasons for leaving.

RAUL: Yes, like rats when the ship is sinking.

They all turn toward the butler.

BUTLER: With these gentlemen's permission, I think the servants left without knowing why. *(He removes his white gloves.)* They were quite happy fifteen minutes before these gentlemen arrived.

Christian is standing next to his wife, Rita.

CHRISTIAN: So, in the end, nothing explains anything. It's extraordinary.

The doctor comes up to calm them all down.

DOCTOR: Keep calm, gentlemen, above all keep calm. Nothing is worse than panicking. A situation like this can't last forever. We're not under any spell. This isn't a witch's castle. *(Leonora, looking sinister and malevolent, goes up to Francisco.)* We can only face this situation by coldly analyzing what's happening to us.

Nobile is very embarrassed. He walks among his guests.

NOBILE: Let me make a suggestion: let's keep quiet for a few minutes. An effort of will power, with the firm intention of getting out of here, to succeed in...

RAUL: Be quiet, Nobile. *(He goes up to him threateningly.)* That's what you'd better do. You're the one who shut us up in this trap; you're the one who made us victims of this bad joke... or whatever it is.

NOBILE: I, my dear friend? I? Because I invited you to dinner? Because I opened my house to you?

RAUL: Exactly! You called us one after an other to ask us to dine here after the opera—"A cordial invitation, dear friends..." *(Simpering)* "Would you do me the honor, etcetera." *(Severely)* We could all have gone home to sleep. Or to the brothel. Anywhere would have been better than here. *(Pacing nervously up and down the room)* Now tell us why you issued this strange invitation?

NOBILE *(dumbfounded)*: Strange? Why? You were all delighted. Even you said how pleased you were by the warm reception you got.

Disconcerted by Nobile's beaten attitude, they nearly all come to Raul's support. Panic-stricken, Letitia comes up to Nobile to support him in case of friction.

RAUL: Well then, let me put it straight and declare—that there is only one person here responsible for this degrading situation, and that person is you!

NOBILE: Me! I think you've lost your mind, Raul.

LETITIA *(to Raul)*: Nobile's right. You're nothing but an idiot!

RAUL: If you weren't a lady...

Letitia holds back Raul, who is about to move away, and violently slaps him twice in the face. Then she moves away, pulling Nobile with her, while Leandro takes hold of Raul and pulls him over to the other side of the room. The door of the closet opens. Roc comes out very discreetly, in his shirt sleeves, closing the door behind him. In the foreground, Leonora is crying in a chair. Francisco and Silvia are next to her.

A GUEST *(off)*: Look at the butler. The water doesn't seem to have done him any harm!

BLANCA *(off)*: I have a headache...

A GUEST *(off)*: No, Blanca, no...

Francisco stands up and nervously walks around the room.

FRANCISCO: But what are the men here doing to put things right? They just talk and talk, like girls. *(He goes up to Silvia.)* Silvia, find a way for us all to leave. *(Angrily)* I'll never set foot is this hole again!

Juana goes up to her brother, who has sat down. She caresses him and turns toward Leonora.

JUANA: Don't be annoyed at his state of nerves. He's more sensitive than a little girl. *(Silvia gets up and moves away.)* I'm sure that no one else is as badly affected by this situation as he is.

At these words Francisco gets up angrily.

FRANCISCO: Don't make me any more irritated than I already am. Can't you see the state of nerves I'm in? I don't want to listen to anyone; I want to be alone.

He moves away. The doctor is leaning over Russell. Beatrice is next to him.

RUSSELL *(with difficulty)*: Happy... I won't see the extermination!

Beatrice is close to Eduardo. Behind them, in the background, Rita comes out of the closet and Blanca goes in.

BEATRICE *(to Eduardo)*: I wouldn't mind dying too, but not like this. Surrounded by people... without being able to be alone with you.

EDUARDO: That's what makes me so mad! Not being able to be alone!

BEATRICE *(low)*: And yet there's a way to cut ourselves off from the others.

EDUARDO *(low)*: Really? It's not possible! How?

BEATRICE *(low)*: I'll tell you when they're asleep... if they ever decide to sleep.

They kiss passionately. Their neighbor, Leandro, is watching them. He looks disgusted. He stands up and moves away. The closet door opens and Silvia comes out and joins Ana, Rita, and Blanca.

SILVIA: I lifted the lid and saw a huge precipice, and at the bottom the clear waters of a torrent.

ANA *(a somewhat lost look in her eyes)*: Yes, and before I sat down, an eagle flew past a few yards below me.

RITA: And as for me, the wind blew a great whirl of dead leaves in my face.

BLANCA: I'm cold.

They separate.

Night. A large porcelain vase near a window in the small drawing room. The camera moves slowly toward the entrance to the larger drawing room and pulls us into the room. Everyone is sleeping or dozing, except for the doctor, who is leaning against a couch watching over Russell. The doctor looks exhausted. He removes his glasses and rubs his eyes. Behind him, Leandro comes out of the closet and lies down on the floor with a blanket wrapped around him.

Close-up of Russell, lying motionless. The doctor's hands cover his face with a blanket. The doctor quietly sits down next to the colonel. The latter is awake and smoking. They both smoke and both talk in low voices.

DOCTOR: Consummatum est!

COLONEL: Already! That's all we need! If only we disappeared when we died.

DOCTOR: They'll be very depressed when they see him tomorrow.

COLONEL: Mr. Roc should have died instead of him. What's one conductor more or less!

DOCTOR: What shall we do?

Silvia comes out of the closet holding her girdle. She lies down next to

Letitia. Eduardo, seeing her lie down, gets up and very discreetly goes to another closet and enters it.

Interior of a closet. Beatrice's face in the darkness. Eduardo lies down next to her. They kiss.

BEATRICE: Did they see you?

EDUARDO: I don't know... I don't know... and I don't care!

The drawing room. The colonel silently goes to the closet, opens it, and takes out a cello, then goes back to the doctor. They both carry Russell's body to the closet. From inside the closet the camera shows them coming in with the body. Close-up of Beatrice, who says nothing. The colonel and the doctor lay the body down in the closet. They both stand up, looking pensive as they overhear the following conversation.

EDUARDO'S VOICE: This is where the sea flows in...

BEATRICE'S VOICE: I can't...

EDUARDO'S VOICE: Lower... There, already... the rictus... It's horrible!

BEATRICE'S VOICE *(passionately)* : My love!

EDUARDO'S VOICE: My death! Oh, my refuge!

The two men look at each other in silence. The doctor gently closes the closet door.

In the drawing room, Letitia is fast asleep, with her head resting on Ana's body. Ana suddenly awakens and sits up. She feels her forehead; she is hot and thirsty. She takes a piece of lemon, chews it, and throws it away. Suddenly her face stiffens and her eyes open in fear. The closet door opens with a squeak, exposing Russell's inert hand. Ana holds back a scream of fear. In vain she tries to waken Letitia, and finally she falls back in a faint.

The boulevard, daytime. The police are holding back a crowd of curious people and preventing them from getting too near the entrance of the Nobile

estate. Two police cars arrive. An officer gets out of one of them. A man goes up to him.

OFFICER: Still nothing?

ENGINEER: What do you expect us to do?

OFFICER: I don't know. But we can't stay here forever.

ENGINEER *(walking with the policeman as they talk)*: Three or four days ago, the mayor, who thought the most important thing was to make contact with the people who are cut off, instructed me to put up loudspeakers so that those who are inside, if they are still alive, could listen and follow our instructions. But he abandoned that idea when I pointed out the absurdity of it.

OFFICER: What absurdity? Why? It seems very plausible to me.

ENGINEER: Well, it would be much simpler than putting up loud-speakers to go into that house, as nothing or no one is preventing us. Yet no one has gone in.

OFFICER: That's absolutely true. *(Pause; the officer lights a cigarette.)* Yesterday we sent in a brigade of sappers in the early afternoon with all the necessary equipment. At nine in the evening they returned to their barracks and not one of them had gone into that house.

ENGINEER: But did they try to go in, officer?

OFFICER: No, and that's what's so serious.

They are standing now near the gates to the estate. In the background several people are trying to break through the police barrier.

VOICE *(off)*: We want to see what's going on inside!

VOICE *(off)*: We're not dogs! Let us through! Death to the police! Come on, let's go.

The crowd has managed to push the police aside. They run past the officer and the engineer and rush toward the big gates of the estate. When they get there, they all stop and look up and down. No one steps through the gate although it is wide open.

A corner of the drawing room. The butler is hitting the wall with an axe in an attempt to uncover the water pipe.

BUTLER *(hitting)*: One... two... three... four...

LEONORA *(off)*: Why are they taking so long? It's so easy!

LEANDRO *(shrugging his shoulders)*: Easy!

Leandro nervously takes the axe from the butler and starts hitting the wall. The pipe slowly appears. The camera shows the floor, onto which cement is falling from the wall; then the guests' naked feet. Everyone is standing around the pipe, except Nobile, who is sitting a little farther away.

SILVIA *(off)*: I have a temperature. Let me through.

RITA *(off)*: Wait your turn.

With worried faces they are all looking at the same thing: the pipe. They all push, trying to get a better view.

BEATRICE: Oh! You stepped on my foot! What's this habit of walking around with your shoes on!

EDUARDO: What's happening? Why are you shouting like that? *(Pause)* All we need is for the people outside to have cut off the water.

BEATRICE *(meanly)*: You should be helping them.

Raul is making his way through to the pipe. He is holding a ball and chain. (The axes and the ball and chain that the guests use are part of a collection of ancient arms that decorate Nobile's drawing room.)

RAUL: Excuse me... excuse me...

Raul carefully takes hold of the spiked ball and aims a blow at the pipe. Worried faces as he strikes. Suddenly, water spouts out. They all rush up. Chaos.

VOICE: Stand aside! Stand aside! Women first!

The doctor is holding them back.

DOCTOR: But... ladies... ladies... my dear friends...

COLONEL *(shouting)*: Didn't you hear?

DOCTOR: Get into line. One glass only at first. Then you can drink as much as you want. It could be dangerous to drink too much water all at once. Especially for the sick. Moderation, gentlemen, moderation!

COLONEL *(pushing Francisco)* : Didn't you hear! The women are first. Go back to your place!

Juana suddenly comes up to her brother and offers him her cup.

JUANA: Here, drink. *(Angrily, to the colonel)* I won't allow you to bully my brother!

Leonora is lying down. Letitia brings her a cup and helps her to drink.

LEONORA: It's so good and fresh!

Letitia stands up. She goes to Ana and gives her some water too.

ANA *(almost delirious)* : Hungry... I'm hungry. Don't eat! Don't leave me alone.

The men are standing around the pipe. The doctor is drinking. Roc has collapsed onto a couch, motionless. Alicia goes to him, lifts up his head, and helps him to drink. She stands up and goes up to the doctor.

ALICIA: Two days without speaking, his eyes closed, cut off from everyone, even me. *(Pause)* And you say it's not serious.

DOCTOR : Let me repeat that, Alicia. *(Very kindly)* He is suffering from the same thing we are. Although at his age it is possible that he's feeling it more...

Rita is standing near the jet of water, sprinkling her face. Beatrice comes up and does likewise, as do Lucia, Silvia, and Blanca.

RITA: Oh, my hands! They're like dead twigs! Perhaps it would've been better if we hadn't found the water. We're only prolonging the agony by drinking.

SILVIA: Well then, don't drink.

Beatrice leaves the group. She walks casually around the drawing room. She sits down next to the butler: he is holding a plate and eating.

BEATRICE: What are you eating?

BUTLER: Paper, madam. *(Close-up of a ball of paper soaked in water.)* It's not very appetizing... but it puts a stop to the hunger. *He offers her the plate.*

BEATRICE: If only it didn't disgust me.

BUTLER: The taste of paper isn't all that disagreeable, madam. My friends and I used to eat it when we were children. Maybe because we were bored at school... I studied with the Jesuits. *(Close-up of a ball of paper as he puts it in his mouth.)* They were good people. We were bored... like most children, I suppose. Paper is good. Apparently it's made from leaves and tender tree bark. It can't do you any harm. *(Insisting)* Would you like to taste it?

LEANDRO *(off)*: Julio! Come here!

BUTLER *(excusing himself to Beatrice)* : With your permission...

Beatrice, pensive, says nothing. The butler stands up and moves away, leaving his plate full of paper balls next to Beatrice, who seems disgusted and exhausted. He goes to Leandro, who is trying to block up the hole in the water pipe as best he can with pieces of cloth. He removes his collar and gives it to the butler so that he can go on with the work.

LEANDRO: Put this rag in...

Ana is sitting on a couch.

ANA *(to Letitia)* : Don't go! Don't leave me alone! *(Letitia leans against Ana, who seems to be delirious.)* Prince! *(Shouting)* Prince!... Our pact!

Francisco, sitting on the floor, is casually shaving himself with an electric razor. Raul passes behind him and unplugs the razor. The razor stops. Francisco says nothing. Raul moves off.

The camera shows Beatrice eating a paper ball and returns to Francisco. Silvia passes behind him and tries to arrange her hair in curls in front of a mirror. Francisco looks at her with disgust. He is a few yards away from his sister, Juana, who is looking at him with ambiguous tenderness.

FRANCISCO: I can't take it! Juana, I can't take it! I swear... I can't stand that harpy who is only combing part of her hair. *(He stands up and goes to his sister.)* I hate her! *(Pause; Francisco seems very much on edge.)* I would rather go hungry and thirsty than put up with her.

Furious at the state her brother is in, Juana stands up and goes up to Silvia.

JUANA *(severely)* : Why don't you comb your hair properly? *(She takes the comb from her and combs her hair roughly and thoroughly, flattening it.)* Like that! You see! Like that! Right through!

Silvia, who is surprised, says nothing, but Francisco takes the comb, breaks it, and angrily throws it on the floor.

Shot of a woman's naked feet. It is Rita, walking. She sits down next to Beatrice.

RITA: Excuse me, Beatrice. *(Very affectedly)* You haven't by any chance seen a little silver box with white pills in it?

BEATRICE: A little box? No, I'm sorry.

RITA: They're Christian's pills. We guard them like treasure. But we're all so confused...

BEATRICE: I'll look for them right away...

Beatrice gets up and moves off. Rita also gets up and goes up to the butler.

RITA *(imploringly)*: Julio, I'm hungry. There wouldn't be a piece of sugar left on the sideboard?

BUTLER *(helpless)*: I'm sorry, madam, but since the day before yesterday there has been nothing whatsoever.

She moves away and joins her husband.

RITA: Do you feel better? Be patient, you'll see that someone'll find it.

CHRISTIAN: I'm sure someone has already found it; and they've hidden it so that I should die. *He starts nervously.*

RITA: Don't say that. *She sits down beside him. They put their arms around each other tenderly.*

CHRISTIAN: You know... *(Pause)* I'm wondering... what they are doing now. I think of them the whole time. *They both look into the distance.*

RITA: I can't forget them either. Our poor children! My only consolation is to tell myself that the father is looking after them, with the same love that we give them!

CHRISTIAN *(angrily)*: The father? But that's exactly what's worrying me—our children are at the mercy of that hypocrite!

RITA: Don't be unfair.

CHRISTIAN: You won't deny that he's courting you, to use a euphemism... but I'd rather keep quiet...

RITA: Don't keep quiet! Talk!

Raul passes behind them. Christian turns around toward him.

CHRISTIAN: Are you interested in what we're discussing?

RAUL: You and your little conjugal problems are the last things in the world that interest me.

CHRISTIAN *(standing up and facing Raul)*: You are most insulting!

And you may have noticed that I've held this opinion of you ever since we've been here.

RAUL *(shrugging his shoulders)* : I couldn't care less. I've felt nothing but contempt for you for much longer than that.

Leandro and Nobile are sitting in a corner of the drawing room. On hearing Christian and Raul arguing, Nobile gets up and goes up to them.

NOBILE *(standing between them)* : Gentlemen, your attitude... I don't know... We're all in the same boat and... we'd all benefit... if we showed a little consideration.

Everyone gets up and surrounds the three men.

CHRISTIAN : You'd do better to keep quiet Nobile.

RAUL : I agree. One has to be pretty cynical to give advice to one's victims.

NOBILE *(surprised)* : Victims? Why? Raul, why? Explain yourself. I would be most relieved if you could give us a good reason.

RAUL *(angered by Nobile's tone)* : I'm fed up with giving you good reasons.

The colonel intervenes. Everyone sits down except Nobile and the colonel, who move away.

COLONEL : Come with me, Edmundo. Don't say any more. Let's not make them any more annoyed than they are already. *(They reach the part of the drawing room where Lucia is seated.)* Sit down.

NOBILE : Please, sit down next to me, Alvaro. *(The colonel sits down between Nobile and Lucia.)* You're my friend. I swear that I'd give my life to end this, to settle this situation. I can't stand unhappiness, and I've always tried to alleviate it. How can they believe that I...?

COLONEL : Yes, yes, calm down now...

Nobile, with a distracted look, stops talking and sits motionless, ignoring Lucia who has amorously taken hold of the colonel's hand.

LUCIA: Alvaro, I'm hungry, so hungry. Think of a way to get us out of this nightmare.

COLONEL *(sighing)*: Only a miracle can get us out of this. *(He suddenly lifts his head to the ceiling.)* Why don't we organize a communal rosary?

LUCIA: Edmundo and I have promised to celebrate a solemn Te Deum if Divine Providence frees us from this trap. *(Pause; Lucia makes a face and holds her nose.)* This awful smell! It's unbearable!

The colonel kisses Lucia's hand.

COLONEL *(off)*: We'll try to do something about it.

As the colonel is speaking, the camera follows his gaze: Eduardo, in his shirt sleeves, and with the help of Leandro and the butler, is blocking up the closet where the dead man has been hidden. They stuff the cracks in the door with wet paper. The butler picks up the pieces of plaster from the hole in the wall, puts them in a silver bowl, and throws them into the small drawing room, just inside the doorway that divides the two rooms. During this maneuver, Ana's delirious voice is heard.

ANA *(off)*: Don't go! Don't leave me alone!

Raul goes up to the double doorway where the butler has thrown the garbage. He kneels and pokes at the mess with his walking stick. He pulls out a cigarette butt with his stick. The camera moves to Letitia, who is standing in front of a mirror. With some satisfaction, she is squeezing blackheads from her nose. Leonora's sickly voice is heard.

LEONORA *(off)*: I'm cold... I'm cold... cold... cold...

Raul picks up the cigarette stub and is happily putting it in his mouth when suddenly his attention is drawn once again to the garbage. He pokes around with his stick and pulls out a little box. He opens it: it is full of pills. He closes it, stands up, and looking around the larger drawing room to

*see if anyone is watching, he throws the box into the small drawing room
and calmly walks back to the middle of the room.*

*The camera follows him as far as Blanca. She is slumped in a chair,
looking haggard, clutching at her hair and pulling it out in lumps. The
doctor takes her hand.*

DOCTOR: Blanca! Your hair! Remember what I told you!

*He moves away and goes up to Silvia, who, with a weary gesture, points
to Leonora who is stretched out on a couch.*

SILVIA: Doctor! What can we do, doctor? Poor thing, she's suffering so much!

They go up to her. The doctor leans over toward Leonora.

LEONORA: I can't take it any more, doctor. Why don't you kill me
and end it all!

DOCTOR: Don't be silly. You've had a good night. Tranquilizers
are becoming as essential as food. *(He stands up as Nobile
comes up to them.)* And to think we haven't even got an
aspirin!

LEONORA *(off)*: Don't leave me alone, doctor, I implore you.
Your presence comforts me. *(The doctor goes back to Ana
while Silvia puts a cushion behind her back. The doctor kneels
down and tries to calm Ana.)* If we ever get out of this... trap,
if I ever get better, I want to go to Lourdes with you.
(Ana's eyes open wider and wider, as though she were demented.)
You promise me, don't you? Don't you?

DOCTOR *(calming her)* : I promise you.

Close-up of Ana and the doctor.

LEONORA: We will prostrate ourselves at the Virgin's feet, for she
is the only one who can get us out of here.

DOCTOR: You musn't talk so much, you musn't get excited. It's
not good for you.

Close-up of Leonora's feverish face pouring with sweat, almost in ecstasy.

LEONORA: When we're at Lourdes, I want you to buy me a washable rubber Virgin. *(Pause)* You will buy it for me, won't you?

She closes her eyes and lets her head fall back onto the cushion.

Nobile beckons the doctor.

NOBILE: Carlos!

They both move away. Nobile takes the doctor over to a chest of drawers and opens it. He takes out a box, unlocks it, and turns around several times to make sure that no one is watching them. He shows the contents of the box to the doctor. Francisco lurks furtively in the background, trying to spy on them.

DOCTOR *(very surprised)*: But... but how did you get hold of this?

NOBILE: We call this drawing room "The Paradise of Thebes." We all get together here sometimes with some friends. We have spent many unforgettable hours here.

DOCTOR: Why didn't you tell me before that... that you had this?

NOBILE: In the present circumstances, just think if the others knew!

DOCTOR: Well! What was used for giving pleasure can now be used for killing pain. *(Looking carefully at the box)* There's laudaunum, codeine, and morphine!

On hearing these words Francisco, who is very interested, interrupts. He looks avidly at the box, which Nobile closes and tries to hide.

FRANCISCO: Morphine? Where?

The doctor pushes him back. He moves away and goes and sits next to his sister, who is seated in an armchair. But he has understood the previous scene.

JUANA: What was it?

FRANCISCO: What's it got to do with you?

JUANA *(insisting)*: What? What's he got hidden there?

FRANCISCO *(evilly)*: You'll see when they're asleep.

The camera shifts to Leandro, who is cleaning a dagger on the table. Letitia and the butler are next to him.

ANA *(off)*: I'm hungry!

Leandro moves off. Blanca passes by.

RAUL *(off)* : Quiet!

The camera returns to Juana and Francisco.

JUANA: That's too much! Be a little more thoughtful.

Blanca sits down next to Francisco, who looks at her with disgust and stands up, holding his nose.

FRANCISCO *(to Blanca)* : You smell like a hyena.

BLANCA *(surprised)* : What did you say?

FRANCISCO: I said that you smell like a hyena, madam.

Blanca leaps up angrily.

BLANCA: How dare you! Why do you insult me?

The colonel goes up to Francisco and looks down his nose at him.

COLONEL: You should be ashamed to talk of such unfortunate things when we are trying to behave like gentlemen and ignore them.

FRANCISCO: Why are you afraid of the truth? She smells bad... like you... like me... like all of us. *(He walks around the room.)* We're living in a pigsty. *(Blanca, in tears, throws herself into an armchair next to Juana.)* Like real pigs! *(Shouting)* You disgust me! All of you! I hate you!

JUANA *(to Blanca)*: Don't pay any attention. He's got a bad case of nerves.

Nobile and Lucia are sitting down. The colonel comes up to them and sits down next to Lucia. He puts his arm around her shoulder. Nobile does not react.

COLONEL *(to Lucia)* : It'll come to a bad end, my dear.

NOBILE *(sighing)* : This is what I've most hated since my childhood! *(He looks around him.)* Vulgarity, violence and filth have become our inseparable companions. *(Pause)* Death would be preferable to living on top of each other in this despicable way.

While Nobile is talking, the colonel, who is next to him, kisses Lucia's hands.

Several hours later. Night. The camera shows the top of a table (quick close-up of a dagger, a glass, a statuette) and moves on to Ana, who is lying down, sleeping fitfully.

Close-up of Ana talking deliriously in her sleep. She sits up like a sleep-walker. Her face is covered with sweat. The ticking of the clock becomes louder. Other strange noises blend in with the rhythm of the clock, in particular the sound of a machine gun. The dark room seems to be devoid of any living being.

The noises (gun shots, creaks) become louder. Ana is terrified at what she sees: the door of a closet in the wall opens. A hand, cut off at the wrist, comes out. The hand, which is very white, slides along the floor.

Ana is panic-stricken. The hand moves across the carpet toward her. She wipes her forehead with her silk scarf, still staring with horror at the hand. The hand goes beneath a piece of furniture, still moving toward Ana. As her fear reaches a climax, she throws her scarf over the hand.

On the floor, the scarf, which is concealing the hand, heaves and struggles. Finally the hand succeeds in disentangling itself and goes back the way it came, still moving along the floor.

Then Ana takes hold of a bronze statuette and leans down threateningly to strike the hand with it. She lashes out once, but the hand avoids the blow and continues on its way. Ana follows it on her knees. She strikes a second time and succeeds: the hand is stilled by the blow. Afraid of what she has done, Ana stands up and goes to sit down on the couch near the table. The noises start up again, particularly the sound of the clock. Close-up of the clock striking three. Various mysterious noises.

Ana is panting, dripping with sweat. She has wrapped her scarf around her again. It starts throbbing violently on her chest. It seems as though her heart is beating violently. She is in great anguish and does not dare look down. The hand emerges from her scarf at the level of her breasts and seizes her throat.

Ana struggles, takes hold of the hand, and throws it on the table. Close-up of the hand, which is still for a moment. Next to it on the table are a glass, a dagger and various other objects. The hand contracts and, crawling slowly toward Ana, prepares to attack again. Ana holds her hands defensively in front of her. She brings them down slowly to the table. Close-up of the three hands. Ana grabs hold of the dagger and strikes the hand, which leaves the frame. Off screen a woman lets out a loud cry of pain. Alicia brings one of her hands up to her mouth and moans. Blanca appears behind her in the room, which is now a little less dark. She takes Alicia in her arms and drags her away. Letitia and the doctor go up to Ana. Letitia lays her down. The doctor seems furious and for a moment almost loses control. Everyone comes up to see Ana.

DOCTOR *(to Ana)* : What have you done? Don't you realize what you've done?

LEANDRO: We must tie her hands.

SILVIA *(terrified)* : Take her away, quick, quick!

LEANDRO: Yes, call an ambulance.

DOCTOR *(to Letitia)* : She has a very high temperature. Put cold compresses on her forehead. And change them every five minutes.

Blanca is trying to comfort Alicia.

BLANCA: Don't cry, Alicia. *(Maternally)* It's all over. We'll watch her to see that she doesn't start again.

Several moments later. Close-up of the doctor's hands opening Nobile's box and handing a pill to Christian, who is lying down, in pain. Rita is sleeping next to him. Christian is surprised.

CHRISTIAN *(sucking the pill)* : It's nauseating, doctor.

DOCTOR *(reassuring him)* : Yes, but it'll relieve the pain and you'll be able to sleep tonight.

As Raul goes up to turn out the lights behind them, Eduardo and Beatrice run toward a closet in the wall decorated with the exterminating angel. They enter the closet.

Interior of the closet. They are lying down. Close-up of their faces next to each other, during the dialogue.

EDUARDO: What day is it?

BEATRICE: I beg your pardon?

EDUARDO: How long have we been here? More than a month, haven't we?

BEATRICE: No, not that long. *(Pause)* We wouldn't have survived without eating.

EDUARDO: I feel as though I've been here forever.

BEATRICE: Me too.

EDUARDO: And that we'll be here forever! Unless...

BEATRICE: Unless?

EDUARDO: Unless we escape together... unless we lose ourselves in the shadows. *(Pause)* You don't answer.

BEATRICE: I'll follow you wherever you go.

They kiss.

The drawing room. Everyone is asleep except Francisco. The camera shows his naked feet walking on tiptoe. He is holding Nobile's box and goes toward Juana.

FRANCISCO *(delighted)*: Look! *(He opens the box and they both look at the contents.)* Just as I thought!

Juana takes the box and sniffs it with pleasure. Raul wakes up and crawls over to them on all fours.

RAUL *(in a low voice)*: What's happening?

Taken by surprise, Juana quickly closes the box and gives it back to Fran-

cisco, who hides it. They both lie down. Disappointed, Raul goes away. The room is in darkness. Everyone seems to be asleep. Roc wakes up and crawls over on all fours toward Letitia with a lecherous look in his eyes.

VOICE *(off)*: Roc!

Roc continues crawling, throws himself on Letitia and kisses her on the mouth. She frees herself and goes back to sleep. Roc continues, goes up to Rita and embraces her in the same way.

VOICE *(off)* : What is it now?

VOICE *(off)* : Be quiet!

Rita stands up. Roc runs back, unobserved, toward the corner of the room where he was before. He pretends to be asleep. Rita cries out.

RITA: Ow! Someone walked on my hand.

Everyone suddenly wakes up.

COLONEL: What? What is it?

The colonel, who was lying down next to Rita, stands up, as does Christian. The two men face each other.

RITA: I don't know. I may have been dreaming.

CHRISTIAN *(angrily, to the colonel)* : I'm not blind, sir!

COLONEL *(not understanding)* : What do you mean?

CHRISTIAN: Your behavior is not worthy of a gentleman!

RITA: Christian, please. You're making a fool of yourself.

COLONEL *(to Christian)* : You'd better watch your words.

They all try to separate the two men.

DOCTOR: Keep calm, gentlemen, keep calm.

NOBILE: Gentlemen, please... what's happened now?

CHRISTIAN: The colonel, like a thief, was taking advantage of the dark...

COLONEL: You scoundrel!

In the closet Beatrice and Eduardo sit up a little to listen to the argument.

CHRISTIAN *(off)* : Let's get this over with once and for all! I challenge you to a duel!

COLONEL: I accept.

Everyone is excited by the challenge. Uproar.

LEANDRO *(tired)*: What a madhouse! They won't even let us rest.

RAUL: Look at him: Nobile in the middle of the fight. Another one of his escapades.

Rita, standing next to her husband, who is clutching his stomach in pain, interrupts.

RITA *(annoyed)*: Can't you see he's in pain?

DOCTOR: You're all mad! Gentlemen, calm down first and then you can settle it. Whatever the outcome, don't let it come to blows. Remember who you are, how you were brought up...

RAUL: What I'd like to know is, did Nobile start this fight?

LEANDRO: We'll have to show him that he can't play with us like this!

NOBILE: I'd rather not answer, gentlemen.

RAUL *(going angrily up to Nobile)*: Yes, but there's a limit to our patience!

LUCIA *(talking about Raul)*: Rita, you're the only one who can calm him down. Talk to him. Calm him down.

RITA: I'll never forget that insult, Lucia. He made me look like a fool.

The colonel moves away and goes to sit down next to Alicia.

ALICIA: Instead of fighting, you'd do better to give us something to eat.

The colonel, who is so angry he cannot contain himself any longer, seizes Alicia and throws her to the floor.

COLONEL: Go to hell, madam!

Letitia watches this scene in horror and rushes up to Alicia, who has col-

lapsed. Everyone comes up to her. The doctor passes in front of the colonel, who is in a daze.

DOCTOR: But Alvaro! How could you...?

The doctor, who is struck dumb by this scene, goes up to Alicia, who is surrounded by Blanca, Letitia, and Silvia. In their midst, Alicia is crying, her face hidden in her hands. The doctor pats her affectionately on the shoulder.

BLANCA: Even the best of us are losing our heads!

Close-up of Leonora, who is delirious.

LEONORA: Please, please, have pity on me...

The colonel comes up to Alicia very humbly and kneels, beseechingly, in front of her.

COLONEL: Please forgive me, madam... you, and all of you... I don't know how I could have... I was beside myself. I'm a changed man. Forgive me, madam, forgive me...

Shot of Nobile next to Lucia and Juana.

NOBILE: May I make a suggestion that you will all, I hope, agree to? In order to avoid these deplorable clashes, like those that have just occurred... *(Pause)* What I want to say is that... I propose that the women sleep on one side and the men on the other.

Most of the guests standing around him seem skeptical. Raul and Leandro are making up.

LEANDRO *(to Nobile)*: Excuse me, but... do you realize that you are speaking to gentlemen?

RAUL *(pointing to Nobile)*: Leave him alone! He's depraved. He takes pleasure in insulting us.

Feeling that the situation is getting out of hand, Letitia goes up to Nobile and addresses them all.

LETITIA *(firmly)*: Edmundo is right.

Letitia turns around toward Nobile to tell him to continue.

NOBILE *(starting again, weakly)*: I thought that... that it would be better for everyone...

DOCTOR *(interrupting him)*: Edmundo, don't go on. *(Angrily)* Don't you understand?

They are all distracted by a strange noise coming from the small drawing room. Close-up of their faces as they stand at the boundary between the two rooms and watch in amazement. The camera moves to what they can hear but cannot yet see: a flock of sheep passing through the hall and going up the stairs, baa-ing. The camera returns to the faces, which show interest. A bear is heard, growling. A scared look passes over the faces.

Shot from the hall of the bear going upstairs.

The sheep trot into the small drawing room and come toward the large drawing room. As they reach the doorway that separates the two rooms, the "shipwrecked" guests open their eyes wide as they become aware of what is happening. They stand aside to let the sheep in, and then block the exit and throw themselves on the sheep with wild cries of joy.

The staircase. The bear continues on up toward a crystal chandelier. The camera shows the chandelier over the staircase, then a bunch of children's balloons outside.

Outside the mansion, daytime. Shot of the balloons, then of the seller, who unties three balloons and hands them to three children accompanied by a priest. The priest pays for the balloons.

In front of the Nobile mansion: crowds; armed policemen; fair-like atmosphere.

PRIEST *(to the children)*: Remember now, you must be very good. *(Going up to the big gate)* Let's go.

A policeman intervenes.

POLICEMAN: Hey! Where are you going?

PRIEST *(humbly)*: Don Christian Ugalde's family. We... just want to look... so that the children can see the house where their parents are..

POLICEMAN *(understandingly)*: Go on.

PRIEST: Thank you. *(He nods. To the children)* Come on!

The group leaves.

Two men are talking to each other near the porch.

PROFESSOR: I know I can go in... talk to them, if they're still alive! Then I can come out and report on the situation to you.

CHIEF OF POLICE: Are you sure of what you're saying?

PROFESSOR: Let me prove it to you.

CHIEF OF POLICE *(shrugging his shoulders)*: Come now...

PROFESSOR: You won't accept? *(As the chief of police walks away, the professor wants to call him back but is held back by a policeman.)* I shall speak to the newspapers, the public authorities. I must be heard; I am absolutely certain I can find a solution to this affair.

The chief of police turns around, shrugs his shoulders, and signals to the the policemen. In the background, the excited crowd near the gate.

CHIEF OF POLICE: Another madman!

The grounds facing the gate: the crowd is massed against the invisible wall. The priest and the children appear. The camera reveals a back view of Christian's little boy walking slowly through the grounds toward the gate, clutching his balloon in his hand.

PRIEST'S VOICE: Keep going, Yoli! Don't stop! *(The child, seen now from the front, has stopped, ill at ease. Behind him, the crowd encourages him to go on; only the priest's voice reaches him.)* Come on, Yoli... Why have you stopped? Go on... don't stop. *(Close-up of the child with tears in his eyes)* Go on, Yoli, go on! Go on! Go on! *(In the background, the priest turns toward the crowd.)* He must go on. Go on, Yoli!

Close-up of the child, who has stopped. He either cannot or will not go any farther.

PRIEST *(off)*: Go on, Yoli! Go on, little one...

The child lets go of his balloon, turns around, and comes back in tears toward the crowd. The priest pats him on the cheek to comfort him.

PRIEST: Why didn't you go on? *(He turns his head toward the assembled crowd and speaks to them.)* Don't ever trust a child!

A WOMAN: Try again.

PRIEST *(pretending to be annoyed)* : Ah! no... no! *(He takes the children away.)* Come, children, we're going.

The large drawing room, seen from the small drawing room, seems to be very smoky. The camera moves forward into the large drawing room. The guests are walking around, coughing and rubbing their eyes. In the fore-ground, Leandro throws wood onto an improvised camp fire. The guests sit around it, relaxed, eating.

A sheep is tied to a piano leg. The sheep turns its head, or so it would seem, toward a large pile of things that have been collected to make the fire. The wool stuffing from the couches and armchairs, a heap of broken objects, a

*cello, etc. are left over. Leandro picks up the cello, smashes it with a mediae-
val battle-axe, and throws the pieces on the fire.*

*Everyone is shown greedily eating pieces of mutton. Suddenly the doctor
stands up and addresses them all amid the sordid mess.*

DOCTOR *(at first, off)* : If we wish to avoid falling into the most
abject and sordid state, we must keep this room very clean
and perfectly tidy. *(Close-up of a woman manicuring her toenails)* We will organize teams to clean up right away.

*Nobile, with a handkerchief tied around his head like a headband, walks
around the room looking disgusted. He passes Alicia, who goes on
manicuring her toenails, Letitia sitting next to her putting on her lipstick,
and Roc chewing the last morsels of a mutton bone. Nobile continues walking.
He passes in front of Lucia and the colonel, who are wrapped in each
others arms. Lucia stops her husband and takes his arm.*

LUCIA : How do you feel?

NOBILE : Fine... My head... hurts a bit...

LUCIA : Poor thing. If you and Letitia weren't here... They are
savages! I'll always be grateful to her for defending you.

*Nobile shrugs his shoulders and continues on his way. The camera shifts
to Blanca, Ana, and Silvia, who are seated.*

ANA : I had a premonition. Before going to the opera that night,
I heard a voice saying, "Take the keys, take the keys!"

BLANCA : The keys?

ANA : In the Cabala, we call all the objects that open the doors
to the unknown, keys. *(Ana opens her handbag and takes out
two chicken claws; she gives one to Silvia, the other to Blanca.)*
Now, Blanca, hold it firmly like that! And you, Silvia, the
other way around, like that.

*Ana shows the two women how to hold the chicken claws: one with the
claws facing upward, the other with them facing downward.*

Quick shot of the room. Raul is shaving the hairs off one of his legs with an electric razor. Leandro passes behind him and unplugs the razor.

The camera returns to the three women: Blanca is reciting strange Latin prayers (the words "in nomine" recur frequently.) Her eyes are raised to the ceiling and she is holding her neighbors' hands.

Behind her, Letitia goes up to Nobile, who is sitting next to the sheep. Without saying a word, she unties Nobile's headband and gives him a dagger, which he looks at sadly as he takes it. Letitia is sitting down, facing him. She covers the sheep's eyes with the headband. The sheep does not put up any resistance and lays its head on Nobile's chest.

ANA *(off)* : I can't read...

The camera shows feathers turning in the air and falling. They fall onto Ana and her companions, who are motionless as though in ecstasy.

ANA: We must have innocent blood... We must wait for the sacrifice of the last sheep.

Francisco is sitting on the ground near a closet in the wall. Suddenly he looks with amazement at his hand, which is resting on the ground: it is covered with blood. He looks at the bottom of the closet and, terrified, goes to join his sister.

FRANCISCO: Juana!

JUANA: What is it?

FRANCISCO *(showing her his hand)* : Look! In the closet...

Catching her breath, Juana gets up and goes to the closet. She opens the door, then quickly closes it so that Francisco cannot see inside. She turns back toward the guests and almost shouts.

JUANA: Gentlemen! My friends!

They all come up to her.

LEANDRO: What's happening?

JUANA *(holding her head)* : There! Eduardo! Beatrice! Doctor! In there...

LEANDRO *(not understanding)* : But what's happened?

Inside the closet. The door opens, the doctor appears and kneels down. Everyone is pushing, trying to see. Silvia laughs hysterically. The doctor stands up and tries to push back the curious people.

DOCTOR: Leandro, and you, colonel, help me. Stop the others from coming near.

They keep back the guests.

VOICE: How did they do it?

Close-up of the dead lovers' faces.

DOCTOR: It doesn't matter. Keep back, please. *(Pushing Lucia)* You too, madam. Come on, now!

The doorway that divides the two rooms, seen from the small drawing room. The guests are pacing up and down in front of the threshold without crossing it. Their faces show amazement and horror as they all watch a strange phenomenon in the small drawing room: the bear is crawling around the room on all fours and growling. Then it escapes up a column. Francisco bursts into hysterical laughter.

LEANDRO *(to Francisco)* : What is it?

FRANCISCO: I was just thinking... *(He goes behind Leandro)* What would you say if I pushed you into the other drawing room?

LEANDRO *(furious)* : Try and I'll kill you!

Close-up of Christian at the doorway between the two rooms. He starts shouting.

CHRISTIAN: Nakam... adenai...!

Across the room, Lucia, the doctor, and the colonel turn around at the sound of his cry.

LUCIA: What does that cry mean?

COLONEL: They've lost what little sense they still had!

DOCTOR: It's the Masonic cry for help. When they hear it, all Freemasons are obliged to go to the aid of the person who uttered it. *(Sarcastically and skeptically)* But here... unless of course the bear...

While he is talking, the camera turns to Roc, who stood up when he heard the cry. In spite of his weariness, he crosses the drawing room and goes to Christian. Roc leans on Christian.

ROC: Christian, the time has come! The word that must never be uttered!

CHRISTIAN: Yes.

ROC: "H."

CHRISTIAN: "I."

ROC *(louder)*: "H!"

CHRISTIAN: "H!"

ROC: "O!"

CHRISTIAN: "H!"

Quick shot of the bear moving around. The camera returns to the two Masons.

CHRISTIAN *(in desperation)*: Oh, no, no, no!

In despair, Christian turns around and goes back to the center of the drawing room supported by Rita. Alicia does the same for Roc. Leandro stands alone at the threshold, looking into the small drawing room. Francisco comes up furtively behind him and pushes him forward. Leandro, who is stronger than Francisco, turns around quickly and punches him in the face. Francisco collapses. Juana takes hold of Leandro by the shoulder and throws herself at him in fury. The two of them are still fighting as Francisco gets up and moves away, laughing.

Juana pushes Leandro to the floor and throws herself on him. They roll around, hitting each other. The others all try to separate them, and after a few moments, they manage to do so. Francisco leans against the mantelpiece, drinks a glass of water, and laughs. His hysterical laughter becomes louder and louder, until it is a mixture of laughter and sobs.

It is night in the drawing room. Everyone is asleep. During the following scene various mysterious noises and voices are heard, coming from outside. The voices don't all match those of the people in the room, but they have the same tonality. A collective nightmare is created by means of images and sounds from the delirious ramblings of each person.

The camera shows Raul's face as he sleeps.

WOMAN'S VOICE: Help!

MAN'S VOICE: Quick, close the windows!

UNKNOWN VOICE: Every man for himself!

MAN'S VOICE: In a moment there will be millions and millions of people in the drawing room.

Close-up of Raul, who shivers without waking up as a woman cries out in terror.

The camera moves slowly to the sound of various incongruous noises. Close-up of Rita sleeping calmly.

RITA'S VOICE: It's late, my little one, come to bed.

Close-up of Rita's hands on her chest.

CHILD'S VOICE: I'm not sleepy.

LETITIA'S VOICE: What a crowd!

The camera continues moving through the room, which is in darkness.

NOBILE'S VOICE: He died in a state of mortal sin!

Close-up of Nobile, sitting with his head resting on his arm, asleep.

DEEP VOICE: "Libera me, Domine, de morte aeterna. Cum de coeli modeli sunt de terrae..."

A choral Te Deum is heard, off. Letitia is lying next to Nobile.

WOMAN'S VOICE *(most likely Blanca's)* : Oh! my child, I shall never see you again!

NOBILE'S VOICE : Look up there... right on top... Can you see him?

Cloudy sky, with a close-up of Raul superimposed. Close-up of Letitia... and snowy wooded mountains superimposed very slowly. The camera moves to the top of the mountains to the sound of bells pealing.

LETITIA *(off)* : The Pope!

NOBILE *(off)* : Yes, it's him... Isn't he solemn and majestic! Like a warrior.

Close-up of a saw cutting through a tree trunk. This nightmare is filmed in very blurred images. As the saw cuts through the tree trunk, we get the impression that it is cutting through a hand, between the index and middle fingers, seen very close up.

The trunk turns into a cello being sawed down the middle. The vibrations of the saw are heard.

A dark sky. Lightning. Thunder. Close-up of a woman's very pale face, rather like a statue. The saw, which has turned into a metal cutter, cuts into the forehead. Flames. Lightning.

Raul wakes up in terror. He clutches his chest with his hands. Close-up of Raul, his eyes wide open.

Close-up of Rita, sleeping with her eyes open. Her lips move.

RITA'S VOICE : Wait, wait, let me fix your pinafore. *(Pause)* Good night, darling...

CHILD'S VOICE : Good night, Mummy...

The camera moves to Francisco, Blanca, and Leonora. Francisco leaves the group and crawls over on all fours to the chest of drawers. He opens it, but as he does not find what he is looking for he closes it angrily and moves on. He finds Nobile's box on the floor. He opens it and sees that it is empty.

He throws it out of the room and collapses wearily near an armchair.

The exterior of the mansion from the boulevard at night. A light-colored flag flaps gently from the top of the porch of the Nobile mansion. In the dark, the chef Pablo and his assistant look toward the house.

PABLO: Nothing. Still the same. It's like a tomb.

CHEF'S ASSISTANT: What about that flag?

PABLO: The house has been put in quarantine. As though there were an epidemic.

CHEF'S ASSISTANT: I'd rather have typhoid!

The two maids come up.

MENI *(off)*: Pablo!

PABLO: Well! What brings you here?

CAMILA: The same as you, Mr. Chef! We came to see if there was anything new.

CHEF'S ASSISTANT: Maybe they're all dead!

MENI: Do you think so?

CHEF'S ASSISTANT: They say that foul smells sometime reach as far as the road.

PABLO: Perhaps the food left in the kitchen has gone bad.

They hear a growling noise and go up to the gate, where the crowd is gathered in spite of the lateness of the hour. They work their way through to the front row. The bear is moving around the grounds. It stands up and shows off. Lucas, the first valet at the beginning of the film, prevents a policeman from shooting.

LUCAS: Don't shoot! Don't... don't.

The bear wanders away toward the house.

LUCAS *(off, shouting)* : Don't kill it! He's very gentle... I'm a servant from the house.

The two valets approach from the boulevard and are surprised to see, in the background, Pablo, Lucas the chef's assistant, and the two maids. They talk as they go up to them.

VALET I *(catching his breath)* : The chef and the maids! Did you tell them we were coming?

VALET II: No, I didn't say a word.

VALET I: Well, what are they doing here?

VALET II: I don't know.

VALET I: Let's go find out... Maybe there's news.

The drawing room. Some are standing, others sitting or lounging. Raul taps Leandro on the shoulder and discreetly beckons him over to an empty corner of the room. He does the same to Francisco and Juana. (The platform that the piano stands on is hidden by a curtain, like a stage in a theater.) The group confers together, then the camera turns to Blanca, Silvia, and Leonora. Behind them, the doctor, who is puzzled, gets up slowly.

BLANCA *(in a low voice)* : Raul said that if Nobile died, this would all come to an end.

SILVIA: When the spider's dead the web unravels...

LEONORA: If he had any dignity he'd know what he had to do.

BLANCA: He's hidden himself with Letitia. *Quick shot of the curtain; then the camera returns to the doctor, who speaks to them.*

DOCTOR: I order you to be quiet. It's the most decent thing you could do. *(Raising his head toward the others who are plotting)* And as for you, gentlemen, you should talk out loud so that everyone can know what you're plotting.

RAUL *(turning around toward him)*: We want to put an end to him.

DOCTOR: Put an end to him? But you're crazy! It's ridiculous, completely irrational.

FRANCISCO: We're not interested in reason. We want to get out of here.

As a precautionary measure the colonel and the doctor climb up onto the platform and, with their backs to the curtain, face the others who are threatening them.

COLONEL: If you're looking for a fight, you'll get one.

The colonel pushes back Francisco, who has rushed up to him.

FRANCISCO: Alvaro!

They are all fighting. The colonel and the doctor put up a good resistance.

LEANDRO: Stand aside! We're got nothing against you or the doctor.

CHRISTIAN: We're acting through necessity.

LEONORA: Kill him!

JUANA: Better late than never!

DOCTOR: Listen to me, you bunch of lunatics!

ANA: Kill the doctor too. If he's against it, there must be a reason.

DOCTOR *(trying to calm them down)*: Think of the dreadful consequences of what you are about to do! *(The doctor does not waver. He raises his voice.)* This evil attempt won't be the only one. *(Pause. He removes his glasses and looks them in the eye.)* It means the disintegration of human dignity. We will turn into wild animals...

RAUL *(pushing him angrily)*: Stand aside, doctor... or I can no longer be responsible for you.

They all come to blows.

LEANDRO: Enough talking!... Let's go!

DOCTOR: Raul, that's enough. Please don't make things any worse!

RAUL: I warned you to mind your own business, doctor...

They are all fighting.

DOCTOR: Enough, Raul!

RAUL: Leave me alone...

In the middle of the fighting the curtain suddenly opens to reveal Nobile and Letitia standing in front of the guests. They all stop and look at the pair in amazement.

ALL: Look, look!... Nobile!

Nobile, who is very pale, raises his arm theatrically to calm them.

NOBILE: Gentlemen, violence is not necessary... There's no point in fighting over something that's so easy to obtain. *(He kisses Letitia's hand and very slowly comes down from the platform.)* Thank you, Letitia.

Nobile very calmly walks around the room and goes toward the chest of drawers, which he opens. He takes out a revolver and very dramatically puts it in his pocket as he returns to the platform.

LETITIA *(off, to Nobile)*: Edmundo! Wait a minute... don't move!

Nobile turns around. The doctor goes up to Letitia.

DOCTOR: What is it, Letitia?

Letitia appears to have made an incredible discovery. The doctor comes up to her. Letitia hardly notices him. During the following speech, which Letitia delivers with great deliberation, the camera follows her slowly as she walks through the room, pushing each person aside, like a sleepwalker slowly waking up.

LETITIA: I don't know... or rather, I do... It's so extraordinary. How long have we been here? *(Pause)* I can't remember. *(Trying to persuade them all)* But think how each of us has changed places during this awful eternity. *(Insisting)* Think of the thousands of combinations, like pawns in a chess game, which is what we were. Even the furniture: we've moved it around hundreds of times... Well, at the moment we're all, both people and furniture, in the same place and in the exact position that we were in that night... or is it another hallucination? Tell me, Alvaro. Answer me, all of you.

First, Rita, Christian, and Silvia.

CHRISTIAN: Well, yes, I was here... and you were next to me, weren't you, Rita? *(Almost stammering)* And on my left...

SILVIA: Me! The same as now.

Alicia is next to Roc, who is asleep.

ALICIA: Yes, and we were on this couch and I was holding your hand in mine...

ROC *(waking up)*: Who... who can remember?

Blanca sits at the piano, ready to play.

BLANCA: After dinner, I sat down at the piano... like this. *(To Letitia)* And you were over there!

COLONEL *(next to her)*: That's right!

Letitia has her back to them.

RAUL: That's all very well... but where is it going to get us?

LETITIA *(severely)*: You were playing, Blanca... can you remember the piece?

BLANCA: Perfectly well. The last piece I played was a Paradisi sonata.

Shot of Blanca at the piano and Letitia beside her.

LETITIA: Well then, play it again, quick. Just the end. *(Urgently)* Didn't you hear me? Play it! Play it!

Juana and Francisco are next to a couch.

JUANA *(to Francisco)*: You were standing behind me. *(The piano is heard off screen.)* Come on, get up.

Francisco obeys his sister and stands up.

On the platform, Blanca is playing the piano. Letitia is leaning on the piano. The colonel is seated in the foreground, listening. The scene is the same as on the previous occasion, except that the people have tired faces and crumpled clothes.

The doctor is standing, listening, with a pensive look on his face. The camera shows everyone in the same position as before. (Raul does not yawn.)

Blanca, at the piano, finishes the piece. Letitia comes up to her and brings her toward the guests.

LETITIA *(shouting at Nobile)*: You were clapping. *(Letitia helps Blanca down from the platform.)* Blanca, you came down from the platform... some friends came up to you...

Without realizing it, the guests re-enact the same movements they performed on that evening several days before. Leandro comes up to Blanca and puts his hand on her shoulder to congratulate her.

LETITIA *(worrying about the outcome)*: Who started talking? *(Shot of Silvia)* Make an effort! Try to remember!

SILVIA *(automatically)*: What a marvelous interpretation!

Nobile, Silvia, and Letitia are next to Blanca. Nobile bows to Blanca.

LETITIA: Answer, Blanca! What did you say?

BLANCA *(looking at Silvia)*: Yes, yes...

NOBILE: What a pity there wasn't a harpsichord. The recital

would have been... *(pause)* would have been... perfect.

Blanca advances through the room like an automaton. Raul comes up to her.

RAUL: Something by Scarlatti now, Blanca... please...

LETITIA *(to Blanca):* It's a little late to go on playing, isn't it, Blanca? *(Accentuating the following words)* It's three in the morning.

BLANCA *(to Raul):* Please excuse me... it's late, and I'm tired...

LETITIA: Yes, we're all tired. *(Accentuating the next sentence)* It's very late and we want to leave. *(She raises her head and*

addresses them all) Don't we, gentlemen?

ALL: Yes... yes... yes...

LETITIA: Well then, let's go! Follow me, all of you! Follow me!
Come on, follow me!

*At Letitia's words they all stand up, embrace each other, and follow her.
She pauses for a moment in front of the doorway that separates the two rooms.
Then, with a haughty look, and with the slightest hint of fear in her
expression, she goes through.*

*She has crossed the threshold. The others push behind her, exclaiming.
They all cross the small drawing room. Francisco and Juana embrace each*

other. The rest of them come through in pairs, holding each other up. The butler switches on the lights, opens the door, and shows them the way.

BUTLER: This way, gentlemen, this way... this way... come on...
this way...

They go out through the second door of the small drawing room. The butler shows the last guest out but stands aside for Nobile, who leaves the room slowly, dragging his feet.

Exterior of the mansion, nighttime. The two valets are near the porch. One of them is drinking greedily.

VALET 1: Brandy from the house! It's good.

Pablo, the chef, approaches.

PABLO: I've only got two bottles left.

In the background, the light over the steps comes on. Lucas comes up and points it out to them.

LUCAS *(almost shouting)*: Look! Light!...

Amazed, the three of them turn around to the maids.

PABLO: Camila... come on!

LUCAS: It's them!

The servants run toward the guests, who are coming down the steps. Instinctively two policemen in front of the steps hold back the crowd.

CAMILA: Oh!... Holy Madonna!...

PABLO: Let's go in.

The chef's assistant joins them.

CHEF'S ASSISTANT *(to Pablo)*: You go first...

They all hesitate for a moment. Finally, the crowd crosses the "impassable" threshold (the servants are first) and go to meet the guests, who are walking with difficulty toward them.

Close-up of the cathedral tower in daylight. The camera moves forward to a bell that swings up and chimes. Off screen a choral Te Deum is heard. Shot of the forecourt in front of the entrance to the cathedral. In the foreground, there is a fountain.

The interior of the cathedral, general view from the entrance: the cathedral is full of worshippers. The altar and the officiating priests are in the background. The camera moves to the altar, where the priest, assisted by two others (one of whom is the priest who looks after Christian and Rita's children), turns around toward the congregation to recite "Ite missa est."

The camera shows the faces in the front row of the congregation in the following order: Silvia, Leandro (the butler is behind them), then Leonora, holding Leandro's arm but with her head leaning on the doctor's shoulder, the doctor, Letitia, the colonel, Francisco, Lucia, Nobile, Blanca, Christian, Rita, Ana, and Raul. Roc, Alicia, and Juana are not there, although one cannot be sure that Juana is not in the background.

On the altar, the priest, who is facing the congregation, makes the sign of the cross. The camera returns to the first row of the congregation and moves across it. Raul and Ana cross themselves and stand up to go. Christian gets up too.

The three officiating priests walk solemnly toward the vestry. At the vestry door they stop. The first priest seems surprised and looks up in the air. The others do likewise. They turn around and look at each other in amazement.

FIRST PRIEST: Why don't we go out after the congregation?

THIRD PRIEST: After them? Why?

FIRST PRIEST: Well... *He shrugs his shoulders and points to the open door.*

The second priest looks at the crowd of worshippers with surprise. They are jostling each other at the entrance of the cathedral but don't go out. The second priest makes a sign to the other two.

SECOND PRIEST: My father...

FIRST PRIEST: Yes?

All three look at the crowd.

SECOND PRIEST: Look... something's happening over there...

At the entrance of the cathedral, nobody goes out.

FIRST MAN: We should wait till they've gone out...

SECOND MAN: That's what I told you...

WOMAN *(going back into the church):* I've forgotten my missal.

VOICES *(amid the chaos):* What's happening?... Why won't they go out?... Let us through!... I'll explain!... You go first!... I'm not in any hurry... That's all we needed!...

The priests are motionless. The crowd of worshippers remains in the cathedral.

Exterior of the cathedral. The cathedral entrance and the forecourt. Close-up of the pealing bells.

A flag is flying from the top of the entrance.

Shots and machine guns are heard. On the town square some demonstrators are rioting. Helmeted policemen are shooting at the crowd. People fall; women shout. There is fighting everywhere.

A flock of sheep advances toward the cathedral. The first ones enter the cathedral as the following words appear on the screen: THE END.

Simon of the Desert *(1965)*

Translated by Anthony Pagden

Credits

Produced by Gustavo Alatriste. Script by Buñuel. Photographed by Gabriel Figueroa. Music by Raúl Lavista.

Cast

Claudio Brook	*Simon*
Silvia Pinal	*Temptations*

The burning sunlight falls upon a cracked and uneven landscape: there are no trees, only thorn bushes and other small desert plants. A group of about a hundred people are seen walking toward us in the distance. They are chanting a psalm and, overcome by the heat, are moving slowly.

The group passes the camera. It is made up of men, women, children, and about twenty monks from the nearby monastery; several soldiers, a centurion, a bishop, two Spanish palmers from Santiago de Compostela, and a grandee of the period, together with a laborer accompanied by his wife and a ten-year-old girl. The laborer is missing both hands. There are also six hooded monks.

The psalm they are singing as they walk could be No. 8:

PILGRIMS: *Domine, Dominus noster, quam admirabile est nomen tuum in universa terra! Quoniam elevata est magnificentia tua super coelos.*

Quoniam videbo coelos tuos, opera digitorum tuorum, lunam et stellas quae tu fundasti;

Quid est homo, quod memor est eius? Aut filius hominis, quoniam visitas eum?

[O Lord our Lord, how excellent is thy name in all the earth! Who hast set thy glory above the heavens.

When I consider thy heavens, the work of thy fingers, the moon and the stars, which thou hast ordained;

What is man, that thou art mindful of him? and the son of man, that thou visitest him?]

The group now climbs a slope which brings them level with the desert plain. Background of cacti. The pilgrims, led by the bishop, the grandee, the abbot, and the other monks approach from the right and disappear, still chanting, behind the plants.

A herd of goats led by a goatherd of extraordinary appearance. He is barely four feet tall and carries a crook with which he drives on the stragglers. His oversized head hardly shows above the backs of the herd. When the pilgrims pass him he runs toward them.

The whole group now arrives, spreads out, and comes to a halt on a patch of sandy ground where two columns, separated by a distance of some forty yards, rise to heights of eight and three yards respectively. On the capital of the latter stands Simon of the Desert, with his arms outstretched and the palms of his hands held up toward the sky. The expression on his face is one of ecstasy; he seems barely conscious of the arrival of the pilgrims. The group forms into two lines, making a bridge between the two columns.

Close-up of the saint, then the camera shifts to several men who have just leaned a heavy plank, with wooden cross-bars, against the smaller of the two columns for Simon to climb down. He has been standing for so long now that his legs will hardly move. Two monks come to his aid; he begins the slow descent.

A few feet away the bishop, Praxedes the rich man, the abbot, and the remaining monks await him. The large column appears in the background with a roughly made ladder leaning against the shaft or the capital. The pilgrims are still chanting.

Simon comes to a halt in front of his superiors. The chant ceases. The abbot comes forward to give Simon the kiss of peace. Praxedes kneels in front of Simon as the bishop begins his address.

BISHOP: *Six years, six months, and six weeks you have stood upon this column, Simon, and your oblation has been an example to all. Go now to this other pedestal, which has been provided for you by the munificence of Mateo Praxedes. There upon your new column you may continue to exhort our brothers by your penitence, following the path that our father, Simon the Elder, has shown us.*

Simon listens impassively, almost with annoyance, for he feels unworthy of the honor. Praxedes goes up to the saint and kneels again.

PRAXEDES: *Take it, Simon, as a sign of gratitude from a family upon whom you have showered happiness by curing me of the terrible sickness.*

Simon blesses him. With everyone following, he begins to walk toward the higher column. The noise of a large number of different voices can be heard.

VOICES: *Simon, pray for us.*

A few of them break through the line of soldiers and rush toward the saint. One of the pilgrims kisses his feet: others try to pull the hair from his arms. Someone cuts a piece from the sackcloth he is wearing. After a struggle, the soldiers succeed in driving them back and Simon continues walking until Zeno stops him.

ZENO: *Wait!*

An old woman comes up to Simon. A pious silence has fallen on the pilgrims.

BISHOP: *Here is your mother, Simon. She wishes to remain near you until the hour of her passing. Let her embrace you for the last time.*

SIMON (to his mother): *Woman, you would have done better to stay home in peace and even, were it possible...*

BISHOP: *Simon, obey and welcome her with joy.*

The mother starts to kneel, but Simon stops her and, embracing her, speaks.

SIMON: *Live near me, Mother, if you so desire, but with my embrace I must bid you farewell in this life. The love I bear you cannot come between the Lord and His servant. Goodbye—when we meet again it will be in His presence.*

Simon leaves her and walks on. He arrives at the base of the column, where the bishop awaits him. The saint kneels and entreats him.

SIMON: *Your blessing, father.*

BISHOP: *You shall have more than that, for you are about to be ordained priest by my hand.*

He turns to Urbicius, who is carrying a white cloth which is wrapped around the chalice and the empty paten. Close-up of Simon's terrified face.

SIMON: *No! No! I am not worthy... No! Not a priest!*

The bishop tries to place his hands over Simon's head and begins the ordination.

BISHOP: *Videte cuius ministerium vobis traditur...* (Simon ducks and takes a step back. The bishop advances toward him.) *... ideo, vos admoneo...*

SIMON: *No! I cannot receive such a blessing... I am an unworthy sinner!*

But the bishop continues to follow him; Simon grabs at the dwarf goatherd's crook as though to defend himself. The bishop thinks for a moment, smiles understandingly, and then gives up.

BISHOP: *Climb your Mount Calvary, Simon, and go in peace... for the moment.*

Simon approaches the bishop again and receives his blessing.

Two women lead Simon's Mother to her hut, which has been erected some thirty yards from the column. They leave her there with a pitcher of water and a basket of food. The women and Simon's mother weep when they part.

Simon has just placed his foot upon the capital of the column. The crowd begins to shout again.

VOICES: *Brother Simon... Blessed Simon... We beseech you to bless us. Guide us in our prayers.*

All kneel except Simon. He stretches his hands out over them.

SIMON: *Pray with me, brothers, pray with me. Our Father which art in Heaven...*

They all reply in unison, repeating his words; but the sound of their response, uttered only by the fifty newcomers, is heard as a roar which seems to come from a thousand throats, like the noise made by the congregation of a crowded church in response to the priest who holds the rosary and intones the Hail Marys one by one.

SIMON (off): *Hallowed be thy name...* (The roar of voices. The camera shows the column and Simon: below, the pilgrims.) *Thy kingdom come...* (The roar of voices.) *Thy will be done...* (The roar of voices.) *On earth as it is in Heaven...* (Simon continues praying with great devotion.) *Give us this day our daily bread...* (The roar is heard off screen. Simon is slightly puzzled; he glances at the crowd but goes on.) *And forgive us our trespasses, as we forgive them that trespass against us. And lead us not into temptation.* (A very brief roar.) *But deliver us from evil. Amen.*

The pilgrims. Now the words of the response are heard.

VOICES: *But deliver us from evil. Amen.*

The man who is missing both hands is praying with his wife and two small daughters. Suddenly the woman stretches her hands out toward the saint.

CRIPPLE'S WIFE (in heart-rending tones): *Look at those stumps that once were hands, the hands that supported our home. Every day we sink deeper into misery. Look on my children, O blessed of men...!*

Simon has listened carefully to the woman; he now turns to her husband.

SIMON (gently): *How did this misfortune befall you, brother?*

The cripple has one of his daughters beside him.

CRIPPLE: *With one blow they cut off both my hands.*

SIMON (off): *But why?*

The girl, who has been following everything very closely, now answers the saint.

CRIPPLE'S DAUGHTER: *For being a thief!*

CRIPPLE: *Yes, it's true... but I repent of my sins. Father, pray that I may be relieved of my suffering.*

The woman beseeches him.

CRIPPLE'S WIFE: *Help us! Take pity on these poor creatures!*

The whole group immediately sets up a clamor.

VOICES: *Help us, Simon... You alone can... Have mercy on the poor.*

Speak the word, blessed Simon.

Simon is seen from below: he raises his arms over the group.

SIMON: *Silence! I can do nothing except pray. Pray with me—but in silence.*

He kneels and prays silently. They all do the same. The monks and the lay brother watch Simon with interest. The pilgrims glance at each other full of anticipation and reverence. The cripple prays fervently with both arms raised. Simon finishes his prayer and crosses himself. He looks down at the cripple.

SIMON (humbly): *Now you are well. Give thanks to God and go about your business.*

The cripple remains with his arms raised. His forearms are out of the picture. He looks up, but his face shows no surprise. He lowers his arms and we see that his hands have been miraculously restored to him, but he himself appears totally indifferent. The same is true of each and every one of the pilgrims. They begin mingling together but with no sign of emotion or even of curiosity. The mother, seated at the door of her hut, is eating an apple she has just peeled. The cripple, his wife, and their two daughters prepare to leave.

CRIPPLE: *Let's go home, Fabiola. I've got to dig the garden.*

WIFE: *We must buy a new spade. The old one's got a broken handle.*

They begin to walk off. The whole group follows; still no one shows the slightest interest in what has just happened.

The cripple's family, walking.

CRIPPLE'S DAUGHTER: *Let's see your hands, father... Are they the same as the last ones?*

The cripple hits her bad-temperedly across the head.

CRIPPLE: *Shut up, you idiot and leave me in peace.*

A little group of three or four people. A young woman addresses an old one.

YOUNG WOMAN: *Take my arm. Your feet weren't made for such rough ground.*

Simon, kneeling, continues to pray without once looking down at those below, most of whom are now leaving. Only the palmers are left; they begin to entreat with the saint and manage at last to rouse him from his trance.

FIRST PALMER: *We have come a long way, blessed one... from Spain, and we wish to receive your blessing before proceeding to the Holy Sepulcher.*

SECOND PALMER: *We also wish to pass the night in the monastery. Is it far from here?*

Simon makes an effort to be kind but he is always annoyed at having his prayers interrupted.

SIMON (pointing toward the horizon): *An hour away—if you walk fast. The abbot will accommodate you with pleasure.*

The palmers kneel.

FIRST PALMER: *Give us your blessing, Father.*

Simon blesses them and then makes a request.

SIMON: *If, on your way to the Holy Sepulcher, you meet with my masters, honor them for my sake.*

The palmers look perplexedly at the saint.

SECOND PALMER: *Who are your masters?*

SIMON (gently): *They are those who are called the poor and the needy, for truly it is they who hold the keys to the Kingdom of Heaven.*

FIRST PALMER: *We will do as you ask.*

They start to walk away. The mother walks by them, carrying a bundle of firewood.

Daniel, Urbicius, and Callinicus, the three monks, stand as unconcerned with the miracle as the rest, watching the departure of the pilgrims.

URBICIUS: *We have spent too much time on these revelations... Let us be going.*

CALLINICUS: *We ought to stay a little longer and accompany Simon in his prayers.*

Daniel solemnly agrees. A woman, who has fallen a long way behind the other pilgrims, now approaches the monks. She is dressed in a coarse garment and carries, on her shoulder, a pitcher which she balances gracefully with her right hand. She is obviously a peasant. Her eyes are bright and smiling.

Simon, cut off from everyone and everything, remains in ecstasy at the top of his column. The three monks kneel and begin to pray. The woman with the pitcher now passes between them and the column. Urbicius and Callinicus remain with their eyes fixed on the ground, but Daniel watches her for a moment. There is nothing wicked about her; she is simply not interested. She walks away.

SIMON'S VOICE (from above): *Where did that woman with the squint come from?*

Daniel looks surprised.

DANIEL: *Squint?... You must be mistaken, Simon.*

Simon looks sternly down at Daniel.

SIMON: *I tell you she had a squint.*

Daniel as seen by Simon.

DANIEL: *Well, I saw both her eyes, and they were both good.*

SIMON: *How do you know?*

DANIEL: *Because I looked, and I saw nothing wrong with either eye.*

Simon's jaw is now set.

SIMON: *And have you forgotten the commands "Do not look upon any woman" and "Neither let her take you with her eyelids" and above all "Do not permit yourself to burn in the fire of vain contemplation"?*

Daniel, afraid and impressed by the tone of Simon's voice, lowers his head. The other two monks continue to stare at the ground. Simon finishes his harangue.

SIMON: *Brother, from this moment on I would rather that you did not come near me until such time as you have taught your eyes to be discreet.*

Daniel bows and begins to walk away, followed shortly by his two companions. The woman, who has walked on without looking back, disappears as though swallowed up by the earth. The mother lights a small fire beside the hut.

The desert. The camera follows Matias, a lay brother of about eighteen. He is extremely clean and neatly dressed. The expression on his beardless face is one of innocence. He is carrying a game bag over one shoulder. In the background is the column with the hermit still standing on the capital. Matias reaches the herd of goats that are watched over by the strange goatherd.

GOATHERD: *Good morning, Brother Matias.*

MATIAS: *May God grant that it be good, brother. Why haven't you brought the milk to the monastery?*

GOATHERD: *Some stinking fox went and breathed his stinking breath all over it and it went sour. I'll bring a fresh pail in the morning.* (They walk among the goats that are cropping the meager grass.) *You going to see the blessed Simon? Yesterday I took him a bowl of curds and a slice of bread only three days old, and damned if he didn't ignore me, the...*

MATIAS: *Don't swear, and forgive Father Simon. He must have been praying.*

The goatherd notices that Matias is stroking one of the goats. He goes up to him.

GOATHERD: *You like that one, eh? She's new. Domitila I call her.* (He strokes her, touches her udders and feels their weight.) *See how firm they are. You only have to touch them and they tremble. The old...*

Matias blushes and the goatherd laughs foolishly. Matias interrupts him and brings the conversation to an end.

MATIAS: *God be with you, brother.*

GOATHERD: *Amen...*

Matias walks away, but he has not gone far when he turns around and shouts, in an admonitory tone of voice.

MATIAS: *And don't be too fond of those animals. Be careful, for the devil's loose in the desert.*

The goatherd, with great conviction mingled with fear, shouts in reply.

GOATHERD: *I hear him at night!*

Simon Stylites standing on the column. He must be about forty years old, but a life spent in the open air and in constant fasting has made him look much older. His emaciated body is covered with cuts, especially on his legs and feet where they are deepest. His hair hangs in long strands, falling almost to his waist. His beard is parted in the middle and reaches to below his chest. The state of his hair is deplorable: the only cure for it would be to shave his head. His dark eyes are ablaze; sometimes they seem implacable, at others gentle. He is dressed in sackcloth, faded by the weather and torn in places. His feet are bare. His dry lips move in prayer, but only a murmur and a few words that are spoken out loud are audible.

SIMON: *Averte iram Tuam... Non potuerunt mihi... cor meum... hei mihi, Domine...* (Pause) *Now I can't remember the end!*

Someone is calling from below. At first Simon does not hear, but the voice is so loud and so insistent that he finally rouses himself from his trance with displeasure and looks down.

MATIAS: *Simon... Father Simon... Here I am. I've brought your food... Blessed Simon, look!* (When Matias realizes that he has succeeded in attracting the saint's attention, he bows.) *The peace of God be with you!*

SIMON (off): *And with you, brother.*

MATIAS: *Today I have brought you bread and oil as well as the usual.*

The mother passes behind Matias, carrying another bundle of firewood.

SIMON (coldly): *My body has no need of these gifts. With water and lettuce, God has provided enough for me to live on.*

He bends over and begins to untie a small leather bag—very much the worse for wear—which is fastened to one side of the column. The camera follows the bag as it descends, and the dialogue between the two men is heard in the background.

MATIAS (off): *The abbot wants you to eat more.*

SIMON (off): *I appreciate his concern, but beg him to forgive me for I know better than he how much I must fast... And you forgive me too.*

The bag has now dropped into the hands of Matias, who begins to open it.

MATIAS: *You know there have been many changes at the monastery. They don't give us wine any longer. Now we have to drink water with cumin seed and pepper. The abbot says it's good for us.*

Simon cannot concentrate on his meditation, and this annoys him. Matias has taken a dry, ant-infested head of lettuce from

Simon's bag. He throws it far away from him in disgust.

MATIAS: *What have you been living on these five days since I saw you last?*

He opens a small water bottle that was also in the bag and smells it, screwing up his face in horror.

MATIAS: *You've drunk also most no water, because this is stagnant.*

He takes three fresh heads of lettuce from his game bag and a sort of small flask from his pouch. He puts them in the leather bag, which the saint begins to hoist up. Simon puts the bag down beside him.

MATIAS (off): *Do you need anything more, father?*

SIMON: *No... Go in peace and leave me to fight.*

MATIAS (off): *To fight!*

SIMON: *How innocent you are not to have realized!* (He is staring down at Matias.) *Son... you are very spruce.*

Matias blushes, taking his master's words for praise.

MATIAS: *Thank you, father!*

SIMON (sternly): *But remember that the cleanliness of the body and its clothing, although innocent enough in the laity, is a sin for all who take up the religious life.*

The silhouette of saint Simon. Below, Matias is standing with his head bowed and his hands crossed over his chest. Simon blesses him and watches him for a moment as he walks away. Matias moves slowly at first, in an effort to appear dignified, but he soon begins to run and jump like a small boy. When Simon sees this he turns his head away in disgust. Furthermore the visit has distracted him and he finds it hard to concentrate.

SIMON (out loud): *Si iniquitatis observaveris, Domine... He's an arrogant fool!... Si iniquitatis... The most abhorrent of your creatures, O Lord, is Man. The very sight of him separates me from You...*

Auxilium meum a Dominum!

He is weak from having stood so long and trembles slightly. He sits down with difficulty.

SIMON (murmuring): *There are no flies today... I'm hungry and thirsty again... I had managed to forget my body, but that wretched child has reminded me of it.*

He picks up the leather bag and opens it. He takes out a head of lettuce, looks at it but, resisting the temptation to eat, returns it to the bag.

SIMON (only his voice): *No... I shall not eat until the sun has risen.* (Out loud) *How far I am from being worthy of you!* (He looks down.) *How tempted I am to go down and feel the mother earth beneath my feet and to run... to run.*

Simon, running like a madman. He stands on his head but collapses when he finds that his muscles are weak and flabby. He reminds one of Don Quixote at Boltenebros.

The mother stacking an enormous pile of firewood.

The column. The saint has his eyes half closed and the expression on his face is one of joyful suffering. A girlish voice is heard shouting in the distance.

GIRL (off): *Here I am, Simon...!*

Simon, roused yet again from his meditation, looks in the direction of the sound but without turning his head. A girl appears, running toward the column. She is dressed in an early-twentieth-century school uniform, and her hair is loose and flying in the wind. She is pushing a hoop before her with the help of a small stick, clutched in her right hand. From a distance she seems hardly to have reached puberty. As she runs she sings to the tune of a nursery rhyme.

GIRL: *Miser Simone, Desinas ineptire.*

Et quod vides perisse, perditum ducas.
Tu praeter omnes une de capillatis.
Cuniculosae Siriae fili.
Simone, opaca quem bonum facit barba.
Et dens Siria defricatus urina.

[Unhappy Simon, put an end to this madness.
And give up for lost, all that is already lost.
You, above all, are the most ragged of men.
The son of a Syrian rabbit.
O Simon, you owe your virtue only to your long beard.
And to your teeth scrubbed in Syrian urine.]

In My Kingdom, Simon,
All who belong are not,
Nor belong all who are.

The girl has arrived at the base of the column. She runs once around it, drops her hoop, and sits on a stone. Seductively she begins to braid her hair. The expression on her face is one of innocence, but she sits with her legs crossed in an obscene fashion, displaying tantalizing underwear (black silk stockings, with velvet garters, above which there is a glimpse of white flesh). Simon looks at her with surprise and distaste.

A clear view of the girl reveals that she is the woman with the pitcher. She has disguised herself as a child in order to heighten her sex appeal. She now pulls up her stockings and fastens them securely with the garters. She smiles warmly at Simon.

SIMON: *What have you come here for?*

GIRL: *To play...!*

SIMON: *Where have you come from?*

GIRL (pointing): *Over there.*

SIMON: *And where are you going?*

GIRL (pointing in the opposite direction): *Over there.*

SIMON: *Who are you?*

GIRL: *I am an innocent little girl, Simon!* (Her behavior is now highly provocative.) *Look at my innocent legs!*

Simon's face looks bored and tired. He turns away from her and begins to pray. The girl laughs, unbuttons her blouse, and displays her breasts, which swell out over her slip.

GIRL: *Look at my virgin breasts!*

The mother, carrying a pitcher, passes the girl without seeing her and walks toward the hut.

Suddenly the girl appears on the capital of the column, sitting almost on top of the saint, who does not even look at her but continues murmuring in prayer.

GIRL: *And look how long my tongue is!*

She pokes out her tongue, but Simon makes the sign of the cross in the air.

SIMON: *I do not fear you, Satan... Christ! Christ!... Christ!*

The girl immediately disappears. There is a loud scream and

Simon looks down to see... the girl gallop away naked on a huge white pig.

GIRL (yelling): *I will return, you tramp, I will return.*

The desert, afternoon. The sun is sinking. Simon's voice is heard intoning one of the ludicrous hymns of the period.

SIMON (off): *Joyous light of the Divine Glory, of the Immortal, Celestial Father and the Blessed, Most Blessed, Jesus Christ, I stand here in the setting sun to praise you...*

The whole column appears on the screen. On the capital Simon continues his hymn.

SIMON: *To the Father, Son, and Holy Ghost. How excellent to be praised by the holy voices of the Son of God.*

The sun now vanishes below the horizon. Simon crosses himself and stoops down to pick up the leather bag. He takes out a head of lettuce and a flask of water. He begins to eat a lettuce leaf, with relish, for he has been fasting a long time. But he sees below... a rabbit that has stopped at the foot of the column. He hesitates for a moment and then throws down the remainder of the leaf. He takes another, chews it, and smiles as he watches the rabbit eat. Then he breaks off a piece of the stalk and stuffs it into his mouth, savoring it with obvious pleasure. He uncorks the flask and drinks avidly but finally restrains himself and, to resist the temptation of thirst, pours away the last drops—not, however, without regret.

The mother drinks water from a pitcher and prepares to bed down for the night on a pile of leaves.

Nighttime. Panoramic view of the desert. The column appears on the screen. Large storm clouds roll across the night sky. Close-up of the saint and the column. Simon is kneeling in an attitude of prayer, with his hands together. A storm is kicking up. Thunder.

Simon from various angles. The wind whistles. There is a dense dust cloud.

A hurricane is in force. Dust nearly blots out the landscape. A deep hollow voice is heard.

VOICE: *The mangy hyena... In the belly of the bitch's daughter... The Blessed Sacrament.*

Simon is desperately holding on to the railing to keep from being blown to the ground. His clothes and his hair stream out behind him. In the dust and lightning, dark and rending voices blaspheme as before.

VOICES: *... the ciborium... God and his Holy Mother...*

Simon's body is in an absurd position, forced almost flat against the capital by the force of the hurricane. Sounds of bleating, the roaring of wild animals, and hollow laughter are heard. Close-up of Simon's terrified face, seen in full in his near horizontal position.

SIMON'S VOICE (shouting): *Dominus, retribuet pro me!*

An apparition approaches swiftly, jolting convulsively from side to side as though it were riding on some galloping wild animal which is invisible to us. A loud clap of thunder. We see a knife, wielded by a hirsute hand, cutting a loaf of bread.

SIMON'S VOICE (howling): *Dominus, exaudi me!*

A flaming cross, crackling loudly, collapses into ashes.

SIMON'S VOICE: *Dominus, diliget justos!*

The saint is still holding on to the capital with both hands so as not to be blown off by the storm. Noise of the wind. Dust swirling.

SIMON'S VOICE: *Christ...! Christ, Lord help me!*

Close-up, night. Saint Simon reinstates himself upon the capital. The wind has dropped. He breathes deeply and crosses himself.

SIMON: *Thank you, O Lord, for having driven it from me.*

The desert, day. The sky, stones, sand, and reflected sunlight. Some twenty monks from the near-by monastery (invisible during the development of the action) are hidden behind a rise in the ground. Some are kneeling, others sitting, but all are listening piously to the saint. Daniel is not among them.

SIMON (off): *For he has said: "Every one that hath forsaken houses, or brethren, or sisters, or father, or mother, or wife, or children, or lands, for my name's sake, shall receive an hundredfold, and shall inherit everlasting life."*

The dwarf goatherd is standing at the foot of the column tying together some pieces of wood to make a ladder. The lay brother, Matias, is helping him. Simon's voice is still audible.

SIMON (off): *In the world I was nothing but a slave, now I am here to be Your slave... It is written that God will help all virtuous men...*

Seated at the base of the column is a monk with the stern implacable face of a fanatic. From time to time he feels the weight of the leather bag, containing the hermit's food, which is hanging from the column within reach of his hand. His behavior is suspicious. He is plotting something. Simon, with his face illuminated, continues.

SIMON: *We shall not rest from our sacrifice. We shall span it like a bridge and, forgetting all that lies behind, shall continue upon our journey until we reach that which is called heavenly, the Eternal Voice... Short are our lives...*

Trifon, the monk who is sitting at the base of the column, is now holding Simon's leather bag. His face expresses indignation at the sight of what it contains.

TRIFON: *Look, brothers!*

They all turn and look at him. Simon stops declaiming and peers down.

Trifon holds up the saint's bag for all to see, and speaks in a shocked voice.

TRIFON: *Look... Our saint is well provided for.* (He takes from the bag a piece of cheese, an apple, a loaf of bread, and a wine skin, which he throws to the monks, one by one. As each item appears) *Cheese... an apple... bread... and wine!* (Sarcastically, imitating the saint) *"We shall not rest from our sacrifice... Span it like a bridge..."*

He laughs. They are all shocked and silent, glancing furtively at one another without knowing what to say or do. The mother, curious to know what has happened, comes out of the hut and joins the group of monks. At last Zeno, the abbot, breaks the silence.

ZENO: *I trust you, Simon. This food must be the devil's work...*

Callinicus, the old monk with a patriarchal beard, speaks to the saint.

CALLINICUS: *Do not do it for me, brother, for I have no need of it, but tell these others, your disciples, why, if you know, that food was in your bag.*

Simon replies modestly and without raising his head.

SIMON: *Calumny is more precious to the devout than loathsome praise, for praise incites pride.*

Trifon stands up and cries angrily.

TRIFON: *Brothers, the hypocrite calls me a calumniator!* (Raising his face to the sky and holding out his hands, he adds in a solemn voice) *I swear before God that I did not put them there.*

Zeno, the abbot, begs the saint.

ZENO: *Blessed one, speak one word and we will believe you... Speak!*

There is a religious silence and an air of general expectation.

Simon, kneeling, raises his arms to the sky.

SIMON: *I am your slave, O Lord. Do with me as you will!*

A triumphant Trifon takes a few steps toward the group of monks.

TRIFON: *You see? He refuses to answer. He's guilty... no one can deny that now.*

The abbot raises his arms for silence. The monks all murmur in protest, but at last they are silent.

URBICIUS (sadly): *One servant of the Lord accuses another, and we who came here for enlightenment find only a disgrace.*

Saint Simon, cut off from everyone and everything, is praying. The group of monks below is growing restless. The abbot intervenes.

ZENO: *Let us now pray to the Holy Spirit, that he may point out the guilty one... We will pray in silence, brothers.*

The mother is sitting on the ground watching a column of ants march to and from the anthill beside her. The abbot crosses himself.

ZENO: *In the Name of the Father, the Son, and the Holy Ghost...*

They all do likewise, except Trifon, whose fingers appear to have been stuck to his forehead. He tugs at them, his eyes open wide in horror, but to no avail. The abbot addresses him in an authoritative voice.

ZENO (off): *Cross yourself, Brother Trifon.*

But it is useless. The lying monk falls to the ground, his body torn by violent convulsions. He foams at the mouth, his teeth clamp shut, and his eyes seem to be about to leave their sockets. The gathering of monks is terrified. Some of them cling together, crossing themselves, others close their eyes. Now Satan begins to speak through the mouth of the possessed.

TRIFON (to Simon): *Castrated pig!... Yes, I put that food in your bag, and I haven't finished with you yet. I won't give up, you son of a bitch, until you blaspheme with your own mouth against the Holy Sacrament and His whore of a mother.*

He has spoken through the foam in his mouth, stumbling and stuttering.

Simon appears not to have heard and continues praying fervently. The abbot, with a stern expression, whispers to Anatolius, who cups his right hand around his ear so as to hear better. Anatolius carries a pouch which holds the holy bread and wine that the monks had brought so as to give Simon communion.

The possessed lets out a loud cry.

TRIFON: *Down with the Holy Hypostasis!*

Zeno, who is still standing beside Anatolius, is roused to holy rage.

ZENO (shouting back): *Up with the Holy Hypostasis!*

The enraged monks take up the cry.

MONKS: *Up with...!*

Trifon goes on twisting around and hurling blasphemies.

TRIFON: *Down with the Anastasis.*

MONKS: *Up with...!*

TRIFON: *Up with the Apocatastasis.*

PETRUS: *Down with...!*

MONKS: *Down with...!*

TRIFON: *Down with Jesus Christ!*

Marcos is a little confused by this flood of "up withs" and "down withs."

MARCOS: *Down with... I mean... Up with!*

Urbicius whispers to the monk next to him.

URBICIUS: *This devil knows more theology than we do!*

A solemn Saint Simon, seen from above, stretches his hands out over the possessed.

SIMON: *In the Name of God I command you to leave the body of this man. Flee, Satan, before the sign of the Cross.*

He makes a cross in the air. The possessed instantly stops twisting and screaming. He lies still. An enormous frog emerges from his body and hops clumsily away.

On the fourth or fifth jump, the frog takes off like a rocket. The camera shows the reaction of the mother to the disappearance of the frog.

The abbot walks over to Trifon, who still has not moved. He looks at him for a moment and speaks sternly.

ZENO: *Let him rest until we go. Then, when we return to the monastery, I will complete the exorcism... in my own way.* (He then turns to the dwarf goatherd and the lay brother, Matias.) *Put up the ladder, brothers.*

They obey him, but with great difficulty, for the apparatus is seven yards high and very heavy. Two other monks come forward to help.

The ladder just reaches the capital. Anatolius goes over to Callinicus and, with deep reverence, hands him the pouch that contains the Eucharist. They open it to make sure that the wine and the bread of transubstantiation, which is wrapped in a white cloth, are perfectly fresh. Callinicus is reluctant to take the pouch. He looks up at the column.

CALLINICUS: *I'm really too old for such heights.*

Anatolius holds it out to Urbicius.

URBICIUS: *I can't do it. I've got gout and my knees won't bend.*

The abbot takes the pouch from Anatolius and offers it to Petrus.

PETRUS: *With your Right Reverend's permission I will refuse... Heights give me terrible vertigo.*

ZENO (severely): *We came here to give Simon the Host, so someone will have to go up.* (He turns to Father Marcos, who is younger and stronger than the others.) *Father Marcos, I know that you will not refuse.*

Marcos looks at the pouch for a moment.

MARCOS: *I will go, but I fear that...*

ZENO: *Fear only God and go...*

The abbot hands him the pouch.

Urbicius speaks to Anatolius in a hushed voice.

URBICIUS: *The abbot could use this in one of his sermons!*

There is an air of great apprehension. Marcos is moving toward the ladder which, for greater safety, is being held by Matias, the dwarf goatherd, and Anatolius. The mother runs fearlessly forward to help.

Up above Simon is lost in prayer. Carefully Marcos begins the dangerous climb. His left hand grips the cross-bars, while in his right he holds up the pouch. They all watch him with rising expectation.

Marcos arrives halfway up the ladder when, with a dry crack, one of the cross-bars breaks in two. Several of the spectators scream. Marcos drops the pouch and grabs, with both hands, at another of the bars. He manages to find a hold on the bar below, thus saving himself from falling. The mother, who has been holding the ladder, opens her arms in time to catch the pouch.

In the background the abbot, with two monks, is watching Marcos—also in the background—climb down the ladder. The mother hands the pouch to Callinicus. The abbot hesitates a moment, then takes a few steps toward the column and addresses Simon.

ZENO: *Simon... It would be wise of us to abandon our task. You saw what happened. But tomorrow we will return with tools to repair the ladder.*

SIMON: *Go in peace, brothers.*

He blesses them. Two of the monks hoist the still unconscious Trifon onto their shoulders; then they all set off. The last to leave are the goatherd and Matias, who, as always, kicks at the stones on the ground, jumps over the bushes, and zigzags back and forth across the path.

The monks walking. Urbicius is the first to break the silence.

URBICIUS: *That Saint Simon! I think, as we couldn't go up, he should have come down.*

Simon cries out after them.

SIMON (off): *Zeno...! Zeno...! Listen to me!*

They all stop and turn to face the direction from which the voice is coming. Matias, the most conspicuous of the group, stands closest to the column. Simon points to Matias.

SIMON: *Put that beardless youth from you.*

Matias looks at the saint with surprise, blushes, and makes a face as if to say, "Why me?" Simon goes on solemnly.

SIMON: *It is not wise for him to live in the monastery, because of the devil's temptations... Tell him not to return until his beard has covered his cheeks.*

The abbot thinks for a moment and then exclaims.

ZENO: *Brother, I am grateful for advice that is so worthy of you.* (Matias is astounded. The abbot walks over to him.) *Matias, when we reach the monastery, you may return home... As soon as you have grown your beard you can come back again... if you still want to.*

Matias is surprised and humiliated; but as he wishes to show that he is obedient, he bows his head. They all continue on their way.

Matias is disheartened. The dwarf walks beside him and, turning to his friend, solemnly repeats the very words that Matias used to him some time back in speaking of the goats.

GOATHERD (referring to the monks): *Don't be too fond of that hairy bunch. Be careful, for the devil is loose in the desert.*

Matias does not answer but shrugs his shoulders in a childish gesture of annoyance. The mother passes them carrying another pile of firewood.

The desert, night. A rainstorm is in progress. The column is in the background. The camera moves toward it and shows Simon under the downpour. The camera then moves back from the column.

Once again a blinding sun falls on the burning desert. At the top of the column, Simon is in ecstasy, his eyes raised to the heavens, his arms outstretched and the palms of his hands spread upward. A dense cloud of flies is circling him. Some settle on his face and neck, others crawl over his parched lips and down his dry cheeks. The saint does not seem to notice.

The sound of soft music, played on oboe and harp, is just audible and grows louder. It mingles with the bleatings of lambs, six or seven of which now advance across the desert.

Simon stands on one foot to rest the other, then reverses the position. He lets his arms fall. His head is heavy and his back aches.

SIMON: *Deus, Deus meus, ad te de luce vigilo, sitivit in te anima mea quam multiplicitor Tibi caro mea.*

[Lord, my Lord, I have kept vigil for you since dawn, and my soul is thirsty and my body also—in so many ways.]

The expression on his face is one of pain, almost of despair.

SIMON: *Lord, Lord... My thoughts drive me from you.*

At this moment he hears the music and, greatly moved, looks about him. His face is full of joy and wonder. He drops to his knees.

A figure, who appears to have walked out of some religious fresco, comes across the desert toward him. He is a young shepherd, with long hair and a curly bifurcated beard; he walks barefoot and with an air of immense grandeur. He is carrying a suckling lamb on his shoulders and is followed meakly by the other white lambs. Simon opens his arms and lowers his head.

SIMON: *Here, O Lord, is the most lowly among your servants.*

The good shepherd draws near.

GOOD SHEPHERD: *You, Simon, are my favorite son. Your sacrifice is sublime. I love you, and dwell in you, and you speak through my mouth.*

Simon is deeply moved.

SIMON: *I wish to die for you, O Lord. I pray you, receive my soul.* (The saint's face grows sad and he asks the vision a question.) *Why are you crying, O Lord?*

Indeed, tears are running down the shepherd's cheeks.

GOOD SHEPHERD: *I am crying for you, my son. Your penitence—your excessive sacrifices—sadden my heart.*

The mother walks past the good shepherd carrying a chicken by the legs. Simon, disturbed by what he has just heard, raises his head.

GOOD SHEPHERD (off): *Stop now, for they do not please me. You must change.*

Simon has begun to be suspicious.

SIMON: *Change...!*

The good shepherd replies in a voice which soon becomes hard and demanding.

GOOD SHEPHERD: *Get down off this column, return to the world and sink yourself in pleasure until its very name makes you sick... Then I say to you, then shall you be close to me.*

Simon stands up full of righteous indignation at the false shepherd's irreverent suggestion. Now he is in no doubt as to who his visitor is.

SIMON: *I do not fear you, Satan! The Lord shall render your guile of no avail. When will you cease to engineer the downfall of the human race, you who before your fall gloried in the Divine Presence?*

The devil puts on an air of mock sadness.

GOOD SHEPHERD: *And if I do repent, Simon, do you imagine that God will reinstate me in my former glory?*

Close-up of Simon's face. It is full of loathing and contempt for the devil.

SIMON: *Never, Satan. Repent if you can, but you will go on like this, century after century.*

Satan's eyes are now ablaze with hatred and malice.

GOOD SHEPHERD: *Now you've made me mad. Well, I'll see that that fat-assed father of yours pays for my wasted journey... and I'm all right as I am, you oaf!*

Satan picks the lamb off his shoulders and throws it angrily to the ground, whereupon it turns into a frog. The same thing happens to all the other lambs. Satan is heard screaming blasphemies.

GOOD SHEPHERD (off): *The filthy Eucharist... In the belly of that daughter of a bitch... Bonum vinum laetificat Hostiam...*

Satan has taken off his belt, which turns out to be a sling. He fits a stone in it and hurls it at Simon. It strikes him on the fore-head. He falls down onto the capital and begins to bleed. The pebbles on the ground around the column, propelled by demonic power, start to fly at the saint. He covers his head with his hands and arms, but his body jerks each time a stone hits him. He makes the sign of the cross in the air.

SIMON: *I exorcise you in the name of Christ. Go, let the just pray in peace.*

Suddenly everything stops. The saint, bruised and bleeding, gets up with difficulty; then he kneels and speaks in a firm voice.

SIMON: *If I fail to free myself from the devil today, O Lord, I shall free myself tomorrow; if I fail in five years I shall wait ten... Continence, prayer, charity, and humility shall be my weapons.*

Suddenly his whole body trembles. He frowns and an expression of terror crosses his face. Something is very wrong.

SIMON: *My eyes must be blind to have mistaken the wolf for the lamb. I have offended you most terribly, O Lord. (Pause. He thinks for a moment, then makes a decision.) I deserve eternal penitence. Until You, O Lord, choose to call me to Your bosom, I shall stand on one leg alone.*

Still bleeding and sore, he begins to carry out this vow and stands on one leg.

The mother, seated at the door of her hut, is weaving a hat.

The sun is just rising on the desert. In the distance is the column with Simon standing on the top of it on one leg. Not far off are the goats and the dwarf goatherd. A lone monk, with his hood thrown back, advances toward us along a path. It is Daniel.

Close-up of Simon finishing a head of lettuce. He swallows the last mouthful and kneels.

SIMON: *Thank you, O Lord, for having given me my food.*

He looks up at the sky. Great dark clouds are rising. A storm is approching. The saint blesses the clouds.

SIMON: *May you make fertile the earth that gives food unto the poor, and do not hail.*

He lowers his gaze to the capital and sees a grasshopper that has just landed there. The saint places it in the palm of his left hand and murmurs his blessing.

SIMON: *I bless you because you are an innocent creature. Go, sing God's glory.*

The grasshopper begins to sing in Simon's hand, then jumps away. Simon looks around him, at the desert and the sky.

SIMON: *What can I bless now? Blessing is not only a saintly excercise, it's amusing and hurts no one.* (He starts.) *What am I saying!*

He hears a voice calling him from below. It is the goatherd, who is carrying a goat in his arms. The herd is farther off, behind him.

GOATHERD: *Father, bless Pelagia.* (He shows him the animal.)

She's very pregnant. Bless her so as what's inside will come out easy.

The saint blesses the goat and then adds another blessing.

SIMON: *And I also give you my blessing, dear brother, for you are poor and meek in spirit.*

For some reason the saint's blessing seems to annoy the goatherd.

GOATHERD: *Don't you go blessing me and my goats in the same breath.* (He pauses for a moment and continues in a gentler voice.) *But I respect and love you, and tomorrow I'll bring you a bowl of milk straight from the goat.*

Simon smiles affectionately at the goatherd's simplicity.

SIMON: *Thank you, my son, but you know that it is useless.*

The goatherd scratches his head thoughtfully.

GOATHERD: *I don't think you're quite right up here.* (He taps his head.) *Must be all this fresh air.*

Simon begins, slowly and carefully, to explain, as though he were addressing a chapter in his monastery.

SIMON: *Believe me, brother, that I eat and drink all I need. I am not a pure unfettered spirit but a man who bears his earthly covering with pain... As for my other need—to discharge—my excrement is like your goats', for my body is withered.*

The goatherd has been listening with his mouth open, and as soon as the saint has finished he shouts.

GOATHERD: *I didn't understand a word of what you said except "withered."*

The goatherd shrugs his shoulder and walks away toward his herd.

The saint smiles sanctimoniously and then gets up again on one leg. His mind wanders for a moment and, without thinking what he is doing, he puts his finger into his mouth and removes a piece of lettuce that had stuck to his gums. He looks at it and idly moves his right hand. Is he, absentmindedly, going to bless it? But he pulls himself up and throws it away.

The mother, on her knees, blows at the embers of the fire beneath her bubbling cauldron.

Daniel is now seen climbing nimbly up the ladder that the monks have left leaning against the column. When he reaches the top he places one foot on the capital and waits for Simon to notice his arrival. But the saint, still standing on one foot, shows no surprise on seeing him. He calmly sits down on the capital.

SIMON: *What do you want?*

DANIEL: *I have come to ask for your forgiveness and your blessing.*

SIMON: *Who are you and why do I have to forgive you?*

DANIEL: *I am the one who looked at a woman. I am repentant.*

SIMON: *You have done well. Go in peace if God has pardoned you.*

Daniel hesitates for a moment. The meeting seems to have ended rather abruptly.

DANIEL: *Before I go, let me give you some news. There is little rest for the servants of God.* (Simon is unmoved.) *The armies of the Antichrist are marching on Rome... Soon they may even reach here.*

SIMON: *Blessed be defeat, if it helps us to win God's glory.* (He thinks for a moment.) *Men are always engaged in fratricidal wars.*

DANIEL: *It's the curse of "mine" and "thine."*

SIMON: *What are you talking about?*

DANIEL: *I'm saying that man fights to defend what he considers to be his own or to take something from another.*

Simon considers this for a moment. He is puzzled.

SIMON (uncomprehendingly): *I do not understand…*

Daniel has understood the moral of the hermit on a column.

DANIEL: *Look… I'll make you understand. This is your bag. Right?* (Simon agrees feebly.) *Now you will see that all I have to do is deny it and we shall begin to argue. Shall we try?* (Simon looks at him with surprise. Daniel speaks aggressively.) *Simon, this bag is mine!* (The saint does not react. In a low voice) *Go on, say it's yours. Argue with me.*

SIMON (half-heartedly): *It's mine…*

DANIEL (violently): *I tell you it's mine!*

SIMON (with great sincerity and complete indifference): *Take it, then...*

Unconcerned by either the problem or its implications, and forgetting both Daniel and the bag, Simon kneels and begins to pray. His companion looks at him affectionately and, without another word, begins to climb back down the ladder.

Daniel passes by the hut where the mother is sitting at the door, tentatively drinking soup from the cauldron with a spoon.

It is nighttime. Heavy snow is falling over the desert. The column can only be glimpsed through the storm. The camera moves toward it to reveal the saint kneeling. The snow has been piling up on his head and shoulders.

SIMON'S VOICE (with annoyance): *I'm cold... cold... Ave Caesar, morituri te salutant... What am I saying! Ave Dominus, take me to your bosom...!* (He has stripped to the waist and the band of knotted wire he wears like a belt is now visible.) *They're calling me from the hearth... A little hot soup... No, no, I don't want it. Angelus nunciavit Maria... What am I thinking of now? Forgive me, beloved mother... Let me have some hot soup!*

A ravine in the desert formed by a dried-out river bed. A bizarre object, propelled by some mysterious force, is seen bouncing toward us in the distance. It soon turns out to be a crudely painted wooden coffin. It passes in front of the camera, slides between thorn bushes like some fantastic animal, and finally comes to rest a few yards from the column. Simon, who has been watching this strange phenomenon, now looks at the funereal object with disgust.

Close-up of the coffin. Little by little, and indistinctly at first, a body takes shape beside it. The apparition is recognizable as the satanic specter already seen before as a woman. He is now dressed in a wide robe; his face is covered by curly black hair and his eyes glint evilly.

SPECTER: *I'm here again... blessed one.* (He laughs.)

Simon raises his eyes to the sky with deep loathing.

SIMON: *Help me, O Lord!*

SPECTER (off): *I promised I would return... and this time is the last!*

SIMON (wearily making the sign of the cross): *Vade retro Satan!*

The specter begins to laugh.

SPECTER: *No vade, no retro, no nothing. I'm staying.* (He points to the coffin and goes on, mockingly.) *Simon, I want you to do me a small favor... If you agree I will leave you in peace forever. Look...* (The lid of the coffin slowly opens and inside is the corpse of the goatherd.) *This dear son of mine, who was born of an incestuous union that I blessed, died yesterday. I want you to raise him from the dead...* (He points at the sky.) *If He will let you...*

Simon replies in a thundering voice.

SIMON: *Vile spirit of darkness! If the Lord allows you to torment me I shall bear it but you shall gain nothing... You revolt me... I can smell the stench of your breath from here!*

The specter looks surprised.

SPECTER: *Of my breath!* (He points to the corpse.) *The stench is coming from him.* (He suddenly grows angry and stamps his foot on the ground.) *You won't raise him, eh?* (When Simon says nothing, the specter stretches out his arms and places his hands on the corpse.) *My son... rise and walk.*

The goatherd's corpse slowly opens its eyes and looks from one side to the other, terrified. He jumps up, out of the box, and runs away. He crosses the path of the mother, who is coming from the opposite direction, loaded down with firewood.

Simon is deep in prayer.

SPECTER (laughing): *I can see you didn't like that.* (Suddenly he appears sitting beside Simon.) *Get ready, Simon, for we are going on a long journey... a very long journey.* (The saint makes the sign of the cross. The specter sneers at this gesture.) *Stop waving your hand around, because this time it will do you no good.* (His voice now assumes an almost friendly tone.) *Simon of the Desert, although this may surprise you, there is really very little difference between us. Since I have enjoyed His company, I also believe in God the Father Almighty, and as for His Only Begotten Son, we shall have a lot to talk about.*

Simon turns his back on his companion and begins fervently to pray.

SIMON: *Credo in Deum, Omnipotentem...*

SPECTER: *Prepare to leave, Simon!*

SIMON: *... et in Christum Jesum, filium eius unicum...*

SPECTER: *Simon... did you hear me!*

SIMON: *... Dominum nostrum, qui conceptus est de Spiritu Sancto...*

The voices of Simon and the devil intermingle, but the devil's is the more audible of the two.

SPECTER: *I'm afraid that they will laugh at you where we're going. You'll have to clean yourself up.*

SIMON: *... natus ex Maria Virgine, passus sub Pontio Pilato.*

SPECTER: *Can't you be a saint without being so filthy!*

SIMON: *... crucifixus, mortuus et sepultus...*

SPECTER: (with annoyance): *Let's go...!*

SIMON: *... tertia die resurrexit a mortuis...*

The specter is becoming very angry. For a short while now, a noise, like that of several approaching motorcycles, has been growing steadily louder.

SPECTER: *That's enough. Can't you hear? They're coming to get us.*

He grabs him by one arm and they both stand as though ready to leave. Suddenly the picture becomes confused and misty. The specter's voice sounds hollow and distorted, as though he were speaking from the bottom of a well.

SPECTER: *We must arrive before the hour of judgment falls upon the world.*

A modern street, daytime. Six powerful motorcycles, of the latest model, appear. They are ridden by "hip" young men, who pass on both sides of the camera at full speed.

The motorcyclists have leaned their machines against the sidewalk in front of a building. They walk into the building, each carrying a musical instrument in a case: saxophone, electric guitars, etc.

Interior of a discothèque. The camera moves back from a close-up of an electric guitar to give an overall picture of the dance floor, where the couples dancing move as one solid mass. Anyone seeing this for the first time might think he was having a nightmare. The neurotic movements, the gesticulations of the dancers—sometimes graceful, sometimes obscene—the contorted bodies, and the imitations of the movements of monkeys, dogs, chickens, etc., all help to make up a disturbing allegory for our time.

A couple advances toward the camera dancing the Chicken Back. Various shots of the Monkey, the Watusi, the Watusi Reverse, and the band. Close-up of a man copying the movements of a Carpenter Bird. Close-up of a woman doing the same.

The camera approaches through the contorted couples until, leaving them behind, it focuses on Simon, who is sitting at a table calmly sipping a Coke. He is dressed in the latest fashion; he is wearing a small beard and his hair is cut in the Beatle style. He is watching the dancing and smoking a pipe. He looks tired and abstracted.

From the edge of the dance floor, next to the mass of dancers, the specter is seen walking toward the camera. He starts in sur-

prise and walks over to the table where Simon is sitting. He is now dressed as a modern girl.

SPECTER: *You here...! What a surprise!*

SIMON: *Hello, you little devil... Sit down... Are you waiting for someone?*

SPECTER: *Yes... an idiot... My boy friend.* (A waiter appears, but before he has time to say anything the specter demands) *A Coke.* (He looks Simon up and down in a friendly way.) *Where have you been, man? Haven't seen you for years.* (He suddenly remembers something.) *And that autobiographical novel... how's it going?*

SIMON: *Like hell! It won't come out right... I'm all hung up!*

The specter replies with mock solemnity.

SPECTER: *The world has lost a great writer!* (He then adds seriously) *And to think that you had so many ideals... and such strong ones!*

SIMON: *La chair est triste, hélas! Et j'ai lu tous les livres...*

SPECTER (laughing): *Now you don't even believe in yourself. That's bad, Simon.* (He sees someone coming toward them.) *Look... Here comes my idiot!*

A boy, dressed in the latest fashion, comes over to them and, without a word, makes a sign as if to say, "Let's dance." The specter gets up and goes with him onto the dance floor.

Couples dancing the Surf. The specter and his companion dancing. A clustered group of girls shaking hysterically. They are all screaming, one of them is crying. Close-up of one who, with an expression of pain, tears open her blouse and displays her breasts. She is almost howling. Another scene of the specter and the boy.

Simon yawns.

The scene shifts to the desert, to the base of the column. The camera moves up the shaft at the same time as it moves away. On top of the column there is now an advertising poster.

The column from the distance. Suddenly it explodes into a thousand pieces in the midst of a great cloud of dust. Against the pieces and the dust appear the words: THE END.

This book was photoset in Baskerville.
It was printed and bound by
Les Presses Saint-Augustin, Bruges, Belgium.

Designed by Jacqueline Schuman.